Helping Young Children to Develop

A step-by-step guide

KIRSTEN SPANSWICK

Jackie Harding and Liz Meldon-Smith

Hodder & Stoughton

A MEMBER OF THE HODDER HEADLINE GROUP

Orders: please contact Bookpoint Ltd, 39 Milton Park, Abingdon, Oxon OX14 4TD. Telephone: (44) 01235 400414, Fax: (44) 01235 400454. Lines are open from 9.00–6.00, Monday to Saturday, with a 24 hour message answering service. Email address: orders@bookpoint.co.uk

British Library Cataloguing in Publication Data
A catalogue record for this title is available from The British Library

ISBN 0 340 720786

First published 1999
Impression number   10   9   8   7   6   5   4   3   2
Year   2004   2003   2002   2001   2000   1999

Cover illustration by Gill Sampson

Typeset by Wearset, Boldon, Tyne and Wear.
Printed in Great Britain for Hodder & Stoughton Educational, a division of Hodder Headline Plc, 338 Euston Road, London NW1 3BH by Scotprint, Musselburgh, Scotland.

Contents

Acknowledgements

Jackie Harding and Liz Meldon-Smith would like to thank the panel of early years specialists who kindly met to trial, advise and comment on the content of this book and whose contribution has been significant. The panel consisted of: Frances Steptoe, Early Years Advisor; Brenda Bowers, Inspection Unit (children), Croydon Social Services Department; Denise Stephens, Nursery Nurse NNEB; Roz Barton, Early Years Teacher; Joy Morrell, Internal Verifier NVQs in Early Years Care and Education; Katie Dixon, student nursery nurse; Louise Boye, Nursery Nurse NNEB; Maggie Mottram, BSc Honours.

We would also like to thank the following individuals and establishments for their valuable contributions to this book: Heath Clark Nursery, Purley Nursery, Ruth Hills and Rutherford School, Carolyn Childs, Carole Blomstrom, Grenville, Samuel and Hollyanne, Roger, Anna, Naomi and Mark and the Child Care and Education Department at Croydon College for their support and encouragement and Dr James Gardner.

PHOTOGRAPHS

The authors and Hodder and Stoughton Educational are grateful to Kimberley Christie-Sturges for providing the majority of photographs shown in this book; also to Letitia Mensah-Dika, Sharon and Gabriella Blunden and Marcel Gilder.

Foreword

As a General Practitioner, I frequently see carers who are concerned about the physical and mental development of their children. Often these worries are due to their own observations but, at times, it is because other people have made comment or have expressed doubts about the abilities of a child. Not surprisingly, these matters can cause a family much distress. We would all prefer our own children to show 'normal' development and may not appreciate the implications of certain special needs.

Therefore, it is vitally important that people involved in the care of a young child have a good knowledge of developmental milestones. It is only with this knowledge that identification of those who are not achieving can take place and reassurance can be given when there are misplaced concerns.

This book contains a concise summary of child development through the early years, with useful hints to enable carers to help children to reach their full potential. It will allow the reader to look after children with confidence.

Dr James Gardner, MB BS DRCOG

Part 1
Studying child development

Aims

To help you to understand:

▶ basic concepts of development
▶ the importance of equality of opportunity in early years worker's practice
▶ a child's right to appropriate care and support
▶ holistic development in terms of understanding the whole child
▶ how norms of development can help you to identify the stages through which children pass
▶ how to use the book
▶ the value of observing
▶ the important contribution parents/carers make to the observation process
▶ the importance of record keeping and planning
▶ the contributions to the assessment process and taking action.

Child watching other children play

Why Study?
- understanding the needs of the child
- understanding holistic development
- understanding norms of development

Theories on Child Development
- introduces a selection of theorists
- briefly outlines some theories
- suggested reading

Observing, Recordkeeping and Taking Action
- the value of observing
- different methods used
- importance of record keeping
- when to take action

ENCOURAGING HOLISTIC DEVELOPMENT

Activities
- the value of observing and assessing
- importance of materials
- role of the adult

**Child Development
Birth to eleven months**
- motor skills
- hearing and vision
- language, cognition and symbolic development
- emotional and social development

**Child Development
Four years to seven years and eleven months**
- motor skills
- language, cognition and symbolic development
- emotional and social development

**Child Development
One year to three years and eleven months**
- motor skills
- language, cognition and symbolic development
- emotional and social development

1

Why Study to Understand Child Development?

Aims of the chapter

To help you to understand:

▶ basic concepts of development
▶ the importance of equality of opportunity in the early years worker's practice
▶ a child's right to appropriate care and support
▶ the importance of observations and assessments in relation to understanding development
▶ holistic development in terms of understanding the whole child
▶ the diversity of social and cultural backgrounds
▶ how norms of development can help you to identify the stages through which children pass
▶ how to use the book.

Basic concepts

Making a difference to children's development

Both the knowledge of child development and the ability to provide a range of activities need to be brought together to match a child's developmental needs. These two areas of knowledge must not be viewed separately and this book will enable you to make the link by showing you how to:

▶ observe and assess a child's development
▶ understand norms of development
▶ plan activities which accurately match the developmental needs of the child.

A child's right

Children are entitled to appropriate care and support from well-informed adults who are experienced in understanding development and in matching activities with a child's individual needs. A safe and secure environment in which to develop is every child's right.

The United Nations Convention on the Rights of the Child contains the following aims:

► the need to respect the rights and responsibilities of parents and guardians in assisting them in bringing up their children;
► to ensure the child's right to privacy and confidentiality;
► to ensure that there is recognition of the child's rights, to express views about his or her own health and treatment and to have those views taken into account in accordance with his or her age and maturity
► to ensure that the child's best interests are the primary concern in making any decision
► to ensure that all services and facilities provided for children conform to the standards of safety, staff and supervision established by competent authorities
► to ensure that all examinations and treatments are necessary and in the best interests of the child and do not interfere with the child's rights to physical and personal integrity.

Equality of opportunity

The Children Act 1989 requires that early years services have policies for equality of opportunity which are reviewed regularly. This means that all staff working with young children should receive regular training and updating in equality of opportunity issues. Early years workers and others who work with children also have a responsibility to promote positive self-images and not make stereotypical assumptions. Early years workers should be prepared to challenge discriminatory language or behaviour and anything else which demeans another person's or child's race, culture, religion, gender or disability.

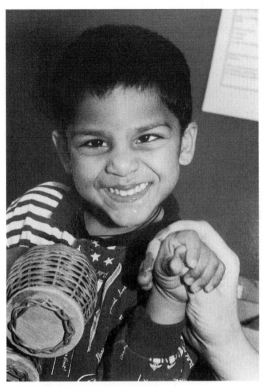

All children have a right to play

Individual responsibility concerning equality of opportunity

Every early years worker needs, to know that positive contributions make a difference in a child's life. This contribution must value and enhance the child's culture, race, religion, gender and disability. If early years workers do not address the issue of equality of opportunity rigorously they will, by default, be allowing a possible situation of hurt, deprivation and disadvantage to continue, thereby hindering a child's progress.

• *Helpful hint* •

CHILDREN WITH DISABILITIES

It is very important to avoid 'labelling' children when discussing children with disabilities. A positive approach must be maintained. The starting point must be what the child can do. For example, a child with Down's syndrome may well follow some of the developmental norms but the speed at which she passes through each stage may be slower. Celebrating individual progress places the child at the centre of the early years worker's plans.

Observations and assessments

The close observation of a child's development in all areas – physical, linguistic, cognitive and symbolic, moral and spiritual, emotional and social – will provide the early years worker with the necessary range of data. This will enable the early years worker to accurately assess the developmental stage of the child, plan suitable activities and judge the effectiveness of those activities and the environment.

Focused observations

The main part of this book covers the usual progress of development of children. While recognising the influence of inherited, social, cultural and nutritional factors, a child may also have particular needs. These particular needs may also be 'special' and could include learning difficulties, special ability or 'giftedness', and difficulty with some aspect of development. A child with a disability is a child first and foremost. Their disabilities are the challenge to the early years worker.

Normal observational activities should be undertaken with all children on a regular planned basis. The initial step of gathering information will involve parents and the immediate team, and may later involve collaboration with the range of staff concerned with the child.

Many children will show variations in development and where variations persist it will become particularly important to obtain a picture of the child's overall development. Early intervention, when necessary, will provide the child with the best opportunity to reach her potential.

The confident practitioner

This book aims to help experienced and less experienced early years workers to make the links between theory and practice and thereby to provide a stimulating environment in which to work.

Early years workers will find it is very satisfying to observe a child making developmental progress as a direct result of accurately targetted activities. They are often surprised at how an activity has made a difference to a child's progress and this in turn has contributed to the early years worker's own confidence as a practioner.

Advice

The examples of 'focused observations' which have been provided usually need to be followed up by specialist advice.

SOURCES OF HELP AND ADVICE

Focused observations and assessments may lead the early years worker to seek professional advice in consultation with the parent/carer. The following people may be able to help:

▶ G P
▶ Health visitor
▶ Teachers
▶ Nursery nurses
▶ Speech and language therapists
▶ Educational psychologists

For further information concerning charities, societies, clubs and other useful addresses contact your local library.

Holistic development

A useful approach to thinking about child development is as a rich tapestry of interwoven threads. Each area of development – physical, linguistic, cognitive and symbolic and social and emotional – represents a multitude of threads. Each child has a unique way of 'weaving' through development.

It is important not to adopt a rigid approach to understanding child development. Please keep in mind this 'weaving' effect when consulting Parts 2, 3 and 4 which give details of the 'threads'.

At the same time milestones are important benchmarks. Early years workers may be the first to be aware if a child appears to be encountering developmental difficulties. The parent/carer may also be aware that the child is experiencing difficulties. Equally, they may be unaware of any difficulty. In addition, they may not be ready to acknowledge that their child has developmental difficulties. The child is likely to make the most improvement in her developmental progress if her difficulty is identified early and appropriate additional support is given. Even children without recognised special needs progress at different rates and not all development is linear.

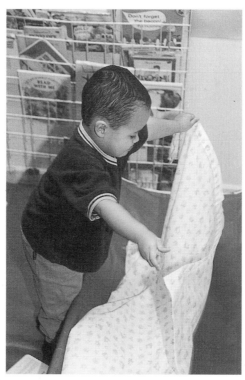

Understanding the whole child

The 'contextualised child'

Until recently most theories about child development have been concerned with 'ideas' about the way in which children develop in the researcher's own culture. Researchers and specialists in child development now discuss the contextualised child. This takes into account not only inherited characteristics but also the enormous impact of environmental influences.

Social and cultural background

The Children Act 1989 states clearly the need to identify the interplay of the child's ethnic background, the child's religion, culture and language and the importance of these influences in assessing the child's needs.

A family's belief about child rearing usually combines cultural and religious traditions and personal preferences. Early years workers must therefore be well informed of the variety of social and cultural backgrounds of the children with whom they work, as well as the wider society. Family patterns and child rearing vary from one generation to another, as well as between cultures. Families will have different ideas about how children should behave, how dietary needs are met and when it is appropriate to introduce weaning, toilet training and discipline, for example.

A well-balanced diet is necessary for healthy development. If a child has a very poor diet, illness may occur and/or energy reserves may become very low. Over a period of time the child's developmental progress will be affected. Children may also become unwell because they are unable to absorb nutrients properly, in which case they will need medical attention.

Children sometimes fail to thrive; their growth may be slow, life seems to be a struggle and they lack sparkle. There are a number of reasons why this may occur and expert advice should be sought promptly. The early years worker needs to be aware of any inherited condition or interruptions to a child's development due to illness or accident so that these can be taken into account during observations and assessments.

As a matter of course, families should be fully consulted about any health matter relating to the child, so recognising the central and informative role of the family. The early years worker must be aware of the cultural customs and issues of language when they seek to understand the information the family gives.

Likewise, any dialogue concerning the child must be understood by the family. If this process of communication is not effective and positive it is unlikely that the child's developmental needs will be fully met – or worse, any difficulty the child has may not be identified early, or at all.

Early years workers need to have an understanding of the meanings that some non-verbal gestures carry in certain cultures. For example, in Japan and some other parts of the world, children are encouraged to avoid looking directly at an adult.

Norms of development

Although there is no precise pattern relating to years and months which we can categorically say all children will follow, we can identify descriptions of stages that all children will pass through. The stages are sometimes referred to as milestones of development and can be given an approximate age-range.

In this book these norms of development are described as 'Approaching X years and over'.

Against this it is important to note that some children may not make this progress at the usual time. Some children are particularly gifted in all areas while others may show a talent in one area, and some children may have delayed development in one or several areas. Early years workers must use their knowledge of developmental norms and how the individual child is developing to judge when a child is experiencing problems. Normative measurements of child development are concerned with general trends and may vary from culture to culture. Researchers are now considering how children develop across different societies and cultures and the common factors across all of them.

Continuous planned observations of a child will provide the early years worker with the essential information which, used against the norms of development, will provide a 'rounded' picture of the child. Caution is needed if, for example, a child achieves one aspect of development earlier than is expected. This does not necessarily mean that they are exceptionally gifted. Similarly if a child does not achieve one aspect of development until later, it does not mean that they should be considered slower. The child is likely to make the most improvement in her developmental progress if any difficulty is identified early. Appropriate support can be given by offering differentiated tasks, outcome opportunities or by altering the grouping of children.

How to use this book

The ideas sections

The purpose of these sections is to encourage:

▶ an activity appropriate to extending the child's development
▶ an opportunity for the early years worker to try out an activity in relation to the child's development.

Theories on child development

We have included a chapter on recent theories of child development which provide a context for both our understanding of the milestones of development and observational work and activities.

He/she

When possible we have referred to children in the plural to avoid confusion between 'he' and 'she'. When this is not possible we have used 'she' to refer to individual children. This is for simplicity only, and is not intended to discriminate against boys.

Make a difference

The early years worker who understands child development, who observes and assesses individual needs and who thoughtfully plans activities can make a difference to a child's developmental progress.

Summary

- ▶ Basic concepts are concerned with making a difference to children's development.
- ▶ Equality of opportunity is the responsibility of all early years workers.
- ▶ A child has the right to a safe and secure environment in which to develop.
- ▶ Observation and assessment is the essential starting point for understanding the child's needs.
- ▶ Holistic development emphasises the interdependence of threads of development.
- ▶ A sound knowledge of social and cultural factors is essential to early years workers.
- ▶ Norms of development help you to identify the stages through which the majority of children pass.

2

Observing How Children Develop, Record Keeping and Taking Action

Aims of the chapter

To help you to understand:

▶ the value of observing
▶ the important contribution parents/carers make to the observation process
▶ the reason for different methods of observing
▶ the importance of record keeping
▶ the importance of planning
▶ the contributions to the assessment process
▶ when it is necessary to take action.

The value of observing

Children present us with numerous opportunities to learn about them. Early years workers need to recognise these opportunities as they arise and use them as the basis for observations and assessments.

The early years workers must always remember:

▶ that confidentiality must be maintained at all times
▶ students need to seek permission before observing children.

It is also important to remember that parents and carers know a great deal about their children through naturally watching them. This knowledge can be invaluable and should be welcomed.

Why Study?
- understanding the needs of the child
- understanding holistic development
- understanding norms of development

Theories on Child Development
- introduces a selection of theorists
- briefly outlines some theories
- suggested reading

Observing, Recordkeeping and Taking Action
- the value of observing
- different methods used
- importance of record keeping
- when to take action

ENCOURAGING
HOLISTIC
DEVELOPMENT

Activities
- the value of observing and assessing
- importance of materials
- role of the adult

**Child Development
Birth to eleven months**
- motor skills
- hearing and vision
- language, cognition and symbolic development
- emotional and social development

**Child Development
Four years to seven years and eleven months**
- motor skills
- language, cognition and symbolic development
- emotional and social development

**Child Development
One year to three years and eleven months**
- motor skills
- language, cognition and symbolic development
- emotional and social development

Different methods of observing

A step on from this 'natural' kind of observing is to plan observations and to analyse what is recorded. There are many methods of observing and keeping records (refer to *How To Make Observations and Assessments*, Harding and Meldon-Smith) and there is a wide variety of terms used to describe each method. The description of the method is more important than its title! Different methods achieve different things. The method chosen will depend on the type of activity being observed and the purpose of the observation. It may be helpful to choose the 'straightforward written account' or 'free description' which is simply written down in the present tense.

Making observations and assessments is a basis for good practice

Good record keeping

Record keeping

Good record keeping must be based only on information which is really useful to store. Early years workers are busy people and record keeping therefore needs to be focused and organised. The introduction of the desirable outcomes has placed a firm focus on planning and assessment. Early years workers use in-depth knowledge of how children develop and learn in order to plan an appropriate early years curriculum. This should be based on sound knowledge of each child facilitated by observing, recording and assessing the child. Record keeping should cover all areas of learning with evidence gathered over time.

The following points indicate the sources of information worth recording:

▶ Records on the child should include:
  - previous records
  - date of birth, address, telephone number and emergency contact numbers, parent(s)/carer(s) names and address
  - significant others
  - arrangements for collection of child
  - any social services or legal constraints
  - current medical information
  - GP name, address and telephone number
  - child's religion
▶ discussions with others involved with the child
▶ discussions with parent(s)/carer(s)
▶ observations of the child's development and behaviour
▶ observations on the child's interests
▶ informative conversations with the child
▶ a portfolio of the child's work linked to the National Curriculum Attainment Targets.

The Children Act 1989 refers to 'the need for well-kept records as essential to good child protection practice'. Record keeping should not be an end in itself. A useful checklist could be: is the record keeping manageable, up-to-date, focused, succinct or useful?

Making assessments

Contributing to the assessment process

It is important that early years workers gather sufficient evidence on which to make an informed assessment. The child may wish to comment or give her own view and these comments can form an invaluable part of the assessment process. The parent/carer may provide essential information which will contribute to the assessment process. Other professionals who are involved with the child may also have important information to contribute.

Evaluating data collected involves consideration of developmental norms and taking into account factors which might influence a child's development.

Planning

The planning cycle involves observation–assessment–planning activities and evaluating the process. Early years workers have to be careful to ensure that what is planned for children is not based on what they think the child may need, but on what they really need. The only way to know this is through careful observational work.

Taking action

'Taking action' covers a range of issues. Providing quality child care practice is achieved by understanding the child's developmental needs and this may mean taking action. Remember the need for confidentiality.

▶ Passing on information is an important part of the whole observation and assessment process but needs to be within the context of confidentiality.
▶ It is sometimes valuable to share information as a result of observation and assessment.
▶ Ensure that the rights of the child are not breached or ignored.
▶ It is important to develop effective communication skills with other child care workers.
▶ An open discussion between parents, carers and workers who have been part of the observation process should be of benefit to the child.

Summary

▶ Observing is an important process in understanding holistic development.
▶ Parents/carers make important contributions to the observation process.
▶ There are different methods of observing to suit different purposes.
▶ Record keeping is an essential requirement of the early years worker's role.
▶ Planning must be based on observations and assessments.
▶ It is important to understand when to take action.

Summary of Part 1

▶ Equality of opportunity is the responsibility of all early years workers
▶ A child has the right to a safe and secure environment in which to develop
▶ Observations and assessments is the essential starting point for understanding the child's needs
▶ Holistic development emphasises the interdependance of threads of development
▶ A sound knowledge of social and cultural factors is essential to early years workers
▶ Norms of development help you identify the stages through which the majority of children pass
▶ Information on how to use the book.

Part 2
Child Development
Birth to Eleven Months

Parts 2, 3 and 4 are designed to enable early years workers to plan activities which will help children to develop. They are arranged in a standard format for ease of purpose but are not intended to be used rigidly.

Aims

To help you to understand:

▶ development in the achievement in mobility, communication skills, understanding of her immediate environment and the beginnings of positive relationships
▶ how to provide a consistent environment which allows her to explore and learn in safety

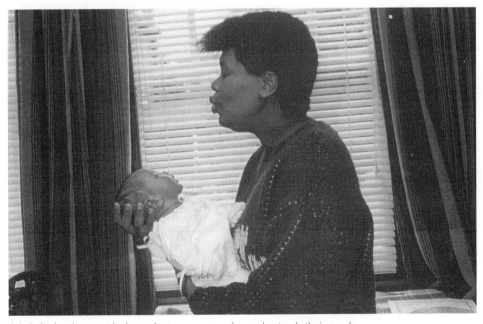

A baby's development is dependent on a carer who understands their needs

Why Study?
- understanding the needs of the child
- understanding holistic development
- understanding norms of development

Theories on Child Development
- introduces a selection of theorists
- briefly outlines some theories
- suggested reading

Observing, Recordkeeping and Taking Action
- the value of observing
- different methods used
- importance of record keeping
- when to take action

ENCOURAGING
HOLISTIC
DEVELOPMENT

Activities
- the value of observing and assessing
- importance of materials
- role of the adult

**Child Development
Birth to eleven months**
- motor skills
- hearing and vision
- language, cognition and symbolic development
- emotional and social development

**Child Development
Four years to seven years and eleven months**
- motor skills
- language, cognition and symbolic development
- emotional and social development

**Child Development
One year to three years and eleven months**
- motor skills
- language, cognition and symbolic development
- emotional and social development

Key issues:

▶ The first year of life sees tremendous development in a baby's achievements in mobility, communication skills, understanding of her immediate environment and the beginnings of positive relationships.

▶ Baby needs sensitive, caring adults who can provide a consistent environment which will allow her to explore and learn in safety.

3

The First Month of Life

Reflexes

A reflex is an automatic physical response to a stimulus. Reflexes occur in all of us, but some are only present in the baby and for a short time after birth.

Rooting

Stroke baby's cheek and this will cause her to turn towards the side stroked as if seeking a nipple with her mouth. Rooting fades by about four months.

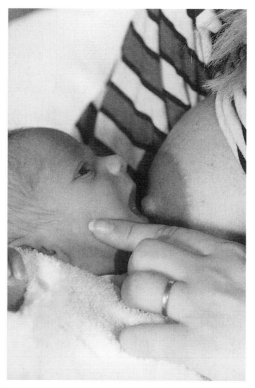

Stroking baby's cheek will cause her to look and turn in that direction

Sucking

Baby will suck rhythmically any object put into her mouth. Rhythmic sucking fades around six months, although babies, children and adults can suck at will.

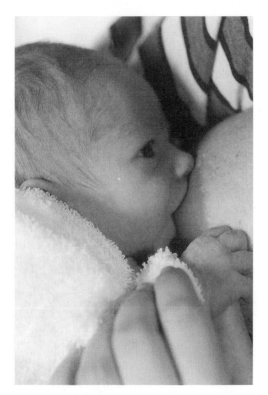

Baby sucks contentedly

Swallowing

Babies swallow in the womb. After birth, babies begin to coordinate swallowing and breathing at the same time. Swallowing is a life-long reflex.

Coughing

Babies will cough if liquid strays into their wind pipe. Coughing is a life-long reflex.

Hand grasp (palmar grasp)

Baby will grasp any object placed in the palm of her hand. The hand grasp fades at about four months.

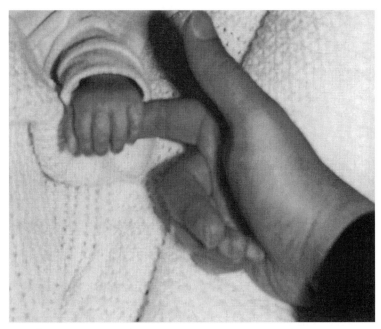

Baby will grasp a finger

Toe grasp (plantar grasp)

Baby's toes curl when the sides of her foot are pressed lightly. The toe grasp fades at about twelve months. Babinski's sign: baby's big toe curls and other toes fan out when the side of her foot is stroked. Babinski's sign fades at about twelve months.

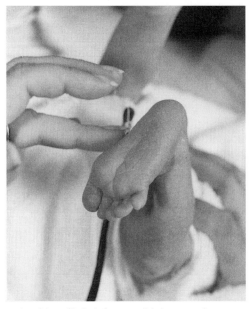

The toe grasp occurs when the sides of baby's foot are lightly pressed

Stepping reflex (sometimes referred to as the walking reflex)

Baby is held upright with the soles of her feet on a flat surface or touching the edge of the table in front. As her feet are brought into contact with these surfaces she makes stepping/walking movements.

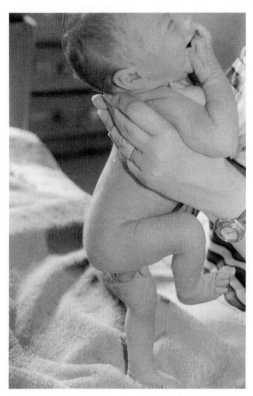

Baby places his feet alternately as if stepping

Blinking

Baby's eyelids close and open again to sudden visual stimulus, for example touching the eyelashes. Blinking continues throughout life to protect, moisten and cleanse the eyeball.

Startle (Moro reflex)

When baby is startled, her arms and legs splay open, she arches her back, and then her arms and legs close as if to hang on to her parent/carer to avoid falling.

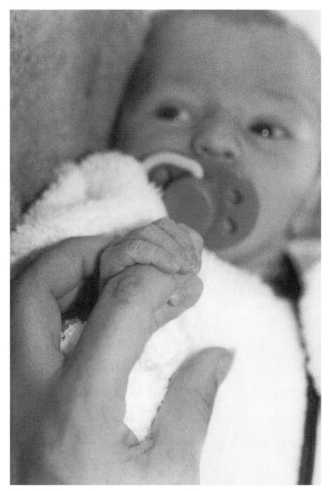

Baby will increase her grip if carer attempts to remove a finger

Motor skills

General posture and movement

▶ baby's head mostly rests to one side
▶ her arms and legs are bent at the elbow and knee **on the opposite side** to the side she is facing
▶ she makes strong jerky movements with her arms and legs
▶ she makes flinch movements while sleeping/resting
▶ her hands are often clenched as in a fist shape, but are occasionally opened
▶ she has no control of her head when lifted to sitting. Her back is curved and her head will flop forwards without essential support

OBSERVATION

▶ note the posture of a new-born baby lying on her back

▶ place your finger in the palm of baby's hand and note the strength of the grasp. With your other hand, stroke the back of baby's hand which is clasping your finger and note how she releases her grip

FOCUSED OBSERVATION

A baby with a physical difficulty, such as cerebral palsy, may be rather 'floppy' or show exaggerated reflexes.

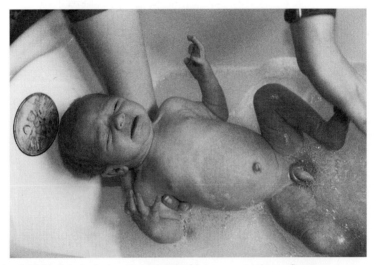

Despite being held firmly baby is demonstrating the Moro – or startle – reflex

ACTIVITY

IDEAS TO DEVELOP MOTOR SKILLS

1 try using a 'womb' tape to soothe baby
2 rock, talk and sing to baby

Vision and hearing

Vision

▶ baby turns her head towards a bright light

▶ she scans near environment with her eyes and tries to fix gaze contrasting light and dark

▶ at arm's length baby gazes attentively at human faces and is beginning to seek eye contact, particularly when feeding

▶ her eyes may follow a toy or shiny object through a range of about a quarter of a circle

▶ a reflex blink is caused by quick movement close to baby's face. This reflex stays throughout life

---

OBSERVATION

Observe a baby in this age-range watching a bright toy moving near to and away from her visual field. Note how she attempts to follow the movement.

FOCUSED OBSERVATION

Babies with poor or no sight will not be seeking to focus

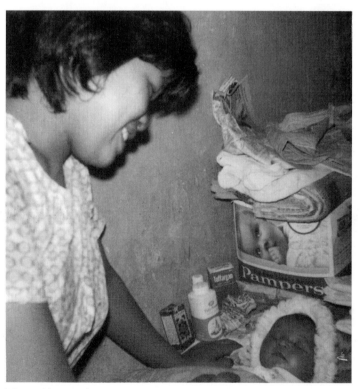

A watchful adult provides security

ACTIVITY

IDEAS TO DEVELOP VISION AND HEARING

1   change the patterns and textures of baby's near surroundings and move baby's position to provide a variety of experiences
2   provide visually and aurally stimulating mobiles and shapes

Hearing

▶ baby is startled by loud sounds
▶ she will quieten to soft rhythmic beat
▶ she turns her head towards her mother's/carer's voice
▶ if baby changes her position suddenly, or if a loud noise is heard, this causes the startle reflex

---

OBSERVATION

▶ observe baby's attention whilst introducing some music
▶ observe baby responding to her mother's carer's voice

FOCUSED OBSERVATION

▶ babies with hearing loss may not show 'startle reflex' in response to a loud sound
▶ babies with hearing loss will make similar vocalisations to other babies at this stage

---

ACTIVITY

IDEAS TO DEVELOP HEARING SKILLS

1   talk to baby
2   sing gently to baby while she settles down to sleep
3   play different tones of music for baby to listen to
4   provide home-made rattles with different tones

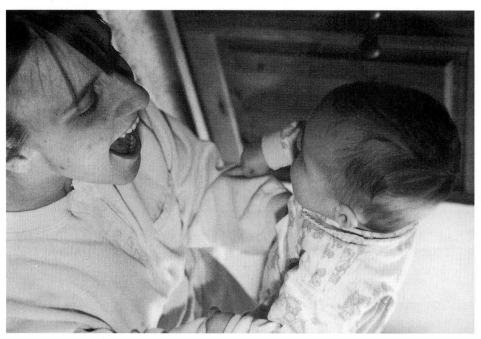

Baby enjoys being sung to

Language, cognition and symbolic development

Language

▶ baby has several different cries
▶ she cries energetically for her needs to be met
▶ she grunts and squeaks when resting (content)
▶ she vocalises in turn with adult

Cognition

▶ baby shows recognition of familiar voices, turns and/or quietens on hearing then
▶ she fixes gaze on patterns, particularly contrasts and facial patterns

---

Observation

▶ observe a baby within the first month of life responding verbally to a familiar adult. Note pitch and tone used

---

> ► show baby three oval shapes: one blank; one with eyes, nose and mouth; one with features scrambled. See if you can tell which one she is most interested in
>
> FOCUSED OBSERVATION
>
> Note any unusual or very high-pitched cry and seek advice.

Social groups provide an opportunity for vocalisation

ACTIVITY

IDEAS TO DEVELOP LANGUAGE AND COGNITION

1 provide a variety of shapes and colours and textures within baby's visual field
2 talk to baby using her name

Emotional and social development

▶ baby may imitate facial movements and expressions
▶ she usually quietens when picked up and may enjoy being cuddled
▶ she is beginning to show awareness of her surroundings

OBSERVATION

▶ observe a distressed baby of this age
▶ note down the strategies of the carer in attempting to calm baby

FOCUSED OBSERVATION

Seek advice if baby is rarely pacified when her needs appear to have been met and she generally appears miserable and distressed.

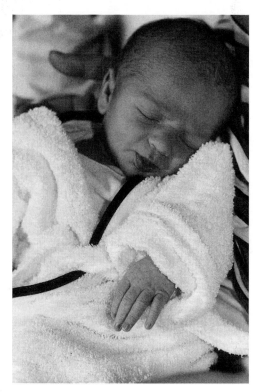

Baby sleeps contentedly

ACTIVITY

IDEAS TO EXTEND EMOTIONAL AND SOCIAL DEVELOPMENT

1 find the position in which baby prefers to be held, for example, in arms for feeding, over shoulder, or in a specially made sling

2 talk to baby during everyday routine procedures, for example, 'Now we'll change your nappy'

4

Approaching Three Months and Over

Motor skills

▶ baby's hands are now half open or open and she can bring them together
▶ when she lies on her back her arms and legs move vigorously – both alternately and together
▶ she can hold her head and neck steadily for a brief period without support
▶ her arms and hands now move smoothly
▶ she has increasing control over her head and neck
▶ when she lies on her tummy she can raise her head and chest and extend her arms
▶ she tries to move with swimming movements
▶ when she is held in a sitting position, carefully supported, she holds her head without a droop but it occasionally bobs and her back is still curved
▶ when she is held in standing position her legs buckle

OBSERVATION

Observe a three-month-old baby reaching for a colourful object. Note the degrees of accuracy of her aim.

FOCUSED OBSERVATION

Muscle tone may vary in a baby with, for example, spina bifida or cerebral palsy.

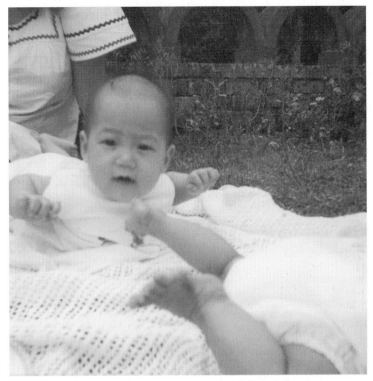

When baby lies on her tummy she raises her head and chest and extends her arms

ACTIVITY

IDEAS TO DEVELOP MOTOR SKILLS

1   place baby on rug or playmat on floor on her tummy with some toys in front of her for a short while. Then bring her to sitting position on your lap with some other toys

2   provide colourful rattles and safe everyday objects, such as a wooden spoon with a face drawn on it

Vision and hearing

Vision

▶   baby's eyes are beginning to focus together some of the time

▶   she uses her eyes to hold adult attention

▶ she focuses on her hands when they are brought together

▶ she watches faces with fascination

▶ she can follow a moving object with her eyes from side to side and up and down

Hearing

▶ she turns her head towards sounds and gives her attention to familiar sounds of food or bath preparation

▶ she responds to her name being called

OBSERVATION

Observe a baby responding to her name being called.

FOCUSED OBSERVATION

A baby with poor vision or no sight may appear to be deep in concentration as she listens and may not react to light.

Baby listening attentively

ACTIVITY

Ideas to develop vision and hearing

1   arrange a colourful mobile which also makes noises of different pitch near enough for baby to enjoy but not touch
2   arrange shiny/reflective objects near enough for baby to see but not to touch
3   change baby's position frequently so that she has different things to watch

•••••••••••••••••••••••••• *Helpful hint* ••••••••••••••••••••••••

Be careful about exposure to ultra-violet light. Always protect babies of all skin tones with clothes and sun protection cream, a wide-brimmed sun hat and a pram shade.

Language, cognition and symbolic development

▶ baby is becoming conversational by crying, cooing, gurgling and chuckling
▶ she varies tone and volume without use of consonants
▶ she is starting to laugh
▶ she smiles and vocalises in response to attention
▶ she cries noisily for needs to be met
▶ she shows an increasing interest in playthings

OBSERVATION

Observe and listen to a baby vocalising:

a in response to adult presence
b alone, unaware of the presence of others.

FOCUSED OBSERVATION

A baby with a hearing loss generally follows the same sequence of vocalisations at this stage.

Baby laughs

ACTIVITY

IDEAS TO DEVELOP LANGUAGE AND COGNITION

1 give baby a rattle or a soft toy to encourage co-ordination
2 introduce finger puppets and sock puppets to encourage communication
3 provide a play centre for baby to gain a response
4 adults can copy baby's sounds, watching and waiting until baby responds, then continue the dialogue

Emotional and social development

▶ baby enjoys all familiar routine and social contacts
▶ she smiles at familiar people as well as strangers
▶ she fixes her gaze on mother's/carer's face while feeding

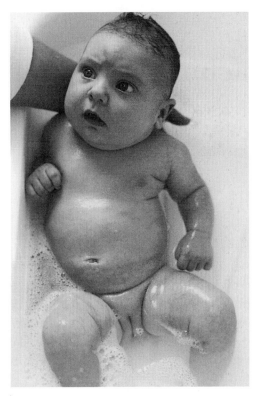

Bathtime is a social occasion

OBSERVATION

Observe a baby during a routine activity, such as bathing. Note pleasurable responses, for example vocal, facial and body movements.

FOCUSED OBSERVATION

Seek advice if baby does not smile.

ACTIVITY

IDEAS TO EXTEND EMOTIONAL AND SOCIAL DEVELOPMENT

1   include baby in a social gathering, such as a family party
2   provide a musical mobile to soothe baby when distressed
3   safe soft toys can provide comfort

5

Approaching Six Months and Over

Motor skills

Gross and fine motor skills

▶ baby supports herself on her arms while lifting her head and chest
▶ she can usually roll from front to back and back to front
▶ she generally shows a desire to be mobile
▶ when she lies on her back she can grasp one foot
▶ she mouths and chews objects and there is an increase in dribbling
▶ she can pass an object from one hand to the other in a palmar grasp
▶ she holds up arms to assist in being picked up
▶ she may sit unsupported for a few seconds and can lean forward to maintain position
▶ her back is straighter
▶ she can take her weight on her legs if held in support
▶ she can support her feeding bottle

• *Helpful hint* •

Never leave baby alone or allow to hold bottle unaided because of the   danger of choking.

OBSERVATION

Observe a baby lying on her back kicking her legs. Note the rhythm and movement patterns.

FOCUSED OBSERVATION

Note any generalised slowing of physical developmental progress in comparison with the progress expected.

Baby dribbles when mouthing safe objects

ACTIVITY

IDEAS TO DEVELOP MOTOR SKILLS

1   provide safe toys for baby to transfer to her mouth
2   allow baby to bounce on your knee and to experience some weight bearing while firmly supported
3   encourage baby to reach and grab toys and rattles
4   water play at bathtime or swimming
5   encourage self-feeding with finger foods

Vision and hearing

Vision

▶ baby reaches and grabs when toys are handed to her
▶ she watches another person's activities
▶ she adjusts her own position to see objects of interest
▶ she fixes her gaze on objects a short distance away
▶ both baby's eyes are focusing in unison and she no longer 'squints' periodically

Hearing

▶ she turns her head promptly to a familiar voice
▶ she babbles tunefully
▶ she responds to routine hearing tests at around eight months of age

---

OBSERVATION

Watch a baby's reaction to a rattle she has been playing with when it falls out of sight.

FOCUSED OBSERVATION

Seek advice if baby continues to squint.

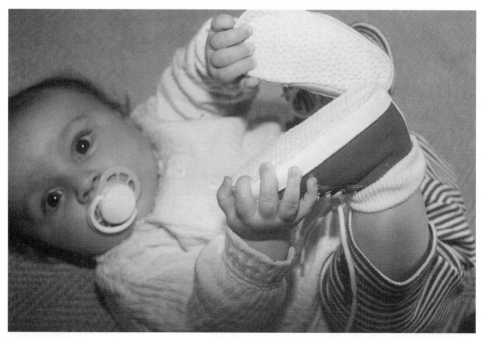

Baby grabs toes

ACTIVITY

IDEAS TO DEVELOP VISION AND HEARING

1 finger rhymes and games – use baby's own hands, for example in 'Round and Round the Garden'
2 provide rattles which make a noise when shaken to encourage sound discrimination
3 musical lights and sound gym to encourage visual discrimination

Language, cognition and symbolic development

▶ baby uses a wide range of vocal sounds in single and double syllables and consonants and makes speech sounds of the language she hears
▶ she laughs and screams and makes some attempts at imitating sounds
▶ she talks to herself in a sing-song voice
▶ she squeals and screams in protest
▶ she uses consonants and vowels combined
▶ she will deliberately shake a toy which makes a noise
▶ she shows an increasing ability to concentrate on objects that interest her, such as bold pictures in books

OBSERVATION

Observe, make a note of and/or tape record all the different sounds a six-month-old makes during a talkative period. Keep these notes for comparison with an older baby.

FOCUSED OBSERVATION

Seek advice if baby seems very passive and disinclined to vocalise.

ACTIVITY

IDEAS TO DEVELOP LANGUAGE AND COGNITION

1 share a picture book with baby, talking about the pictures and turning pages. Books should show cultural variety
2 provide manipulative and table-top toys for exploration
3 show baby some keys/rattle and let her see you hide and retrieve them from under a cloth or cup

Baby finds noisy toys very interesting

Emotional and social development

▶ baby joins in family meals with obvious enjoyment
▶ she tries to imitate sounds
▶ usually she welcomes strangers, but is occasionally shy
▶ she is starting to participate in active games
▶ she deliberately seeks attention
▶ she starts to help with dressing by pushing limbs into clothes

---

OBSERVATION

Observe a six-month-old baby with an older sibling or child.

FOCUSED OBSERVATION

Seek advice if baby seems unresponsive emotionally.

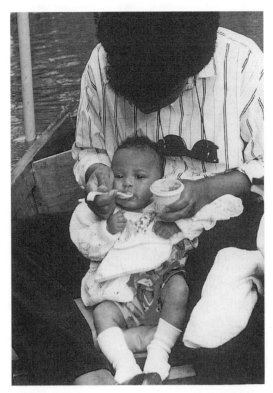

Mealtimes are a social occasion

ACTIVITY

IDEAS TO EXTEND EMOTIONAL AND SOCIAL DEVELOPMENT

1   enable baby to meet other babies or children, especially if she does not have siblings
2   show her pictures of familiar family/friends/pets and talk about them
3   provide baby with different types of textured fabric

6

Approaching Nine Months and Over

Motor skills

Gross and fine motor skills

▶ baby can sit securely without support and with a straight back
▶ she manipulates toys with interest
▶ she may pull herself up by using furniture and stands holding on
▶ she reaches out for a toy
▶ she trys to find ways to move around and is likely to crawl, wriggle along on her tummy or roll
▶ she is starting to grasp objects between finger and thumb
▶ she is able to hold and chew a biscuit
▶ she flaps arms up and down together when excited

•••••••••••••••••••••••••••• *Helpful hint* ••••••••••••••••••••••••

Baby's increasing mobility means that careful observation of baby's environment is needed to remove hazards.

OBSERVATION

Observe baby exploring ways of becoming mobile.

FOCUSED OBSERVATION

Note if baby does not reach up to carer when being picked up.

◦ ACTIVITY

IDEAS TO DEVELOP MOTOR SKILLS

1   place some toys just high enough so that baby can safely pull herself up in order to reach them
2   introduce baby to musical equipment from a range of cultures: steel drums, glockenspeil, for example and help baby to make sounds

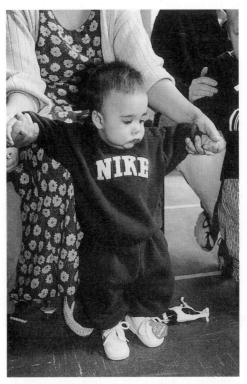

Baby can stand with support

Vision and hearing

Vision

▶ baby can focus on objects on the other side of the room
▶ she focuses her attention on people and local environment
▶ she looks for a toy that has fallen out of sight
▶ she is starting to use her index finger to touch items and to point

Hearing

▶ baby responds to her name being called
▶ she gains enjoyment from rhymes and songs

OBSERVATION

Observe baby's responses to rhymes and jingles.

FOCUSED OBSERVATION

Seek advice if baby does not turn when her name is called.

Baby is interested in reflections which move

IDEAS TO DEVELOP VISION AND HEARING

1   give baby new experiences, such as visiting friends and different places
2   share pop-up and lift-the-flap books with baby
3   sing songs to baby to encourage aural discrimination

Language, cognition and symbolic development

▶ baby enjoys communicating with people she knows
▶ she sounds 'mm' 'gg' 'dd' 'brr' and tunefully babbles
▶ she copies adult cough
▶ she listens between vocalisations
▶ she listens attentively to the voice of a known person
▶ she shouts
▶ she turns to find the source of a sound
▶ she responds to 'no' by stopping

OBSERVATION

Observe and make a note of the different sounds you hear baby make and compare with your records for a six-month-old baby.

FOCUSED OBSERVATION

Note if baby does not appear to enjoy or involve herself with known adults and children who are attempting to communicate with her.

Baby manipulates toy with interest

ACTIVITY

IDEAS TO DEVELOP LANGUAGE AND COGNITION

1   encourage baby to make sounds that she enjoys
2   sing nursery rhymes to her for enjoyment

Emotional and social development

▶ baby enjoys rhymes and songs and social interation
▶ she shows attachment to main carer(s) and, for example, siblings
▶ she is becoming cautious of strangers
▶ she is becoming assertive and can show annoyance by stiffening, sometimes accompanied by verbal protest
▶ she continues to explore objects by transferring them to her mouth
▶ she may become attached to a comforter
▶ she can hold a spoon while eating and enjoys the social occasion of a mealtime

OBSERVATION

Observe a person with whom baby is familiar enjoying a game of peek-a-boo and watch her reactions, enjoyment and laughter.

FOCUSED OBSERVATION

Be alert to baby if she is cautious of all adults including those with whom she should be familiar.

ACTIVITY

IDEAS TO EXTEND EMOTIONAL AND SOCIAL DEVELOPMENT

1   sing action songs and rhymes together
2   play peek-a-boo and seeking and finding
3   call baby by her name
4   provide an activity blanket and help her to explore it
5   provide an activity play gym and respond to her activities and discoveries

Summary of Part 2

▶ The first year of life sees tremendous development in the achievement
in mobility, communication skills, understanding of her immediate
environment and the beginnings of positive relationships.

▶ She needs sensitive, caring adults who provide a consistent
environment which allows her to explore and learn in safety.

Part 3

Child development
One year to three years and eleven months

Aims

To help you to understand:

► how she experiments with her physical capabilities
► how she tries out new skills and ideas
► how new language skills open up new possibilities.

Key issues:

► Watchful, constant supervision is essential as child experiments with her physical capabilities.
► Enthusiastic adults who celebrate the child's achievements will provide a good basis from which the child can try out new skills and ideas.
► A significant growth in language skills opens up new possibilities.

Stimulating toys encourage development

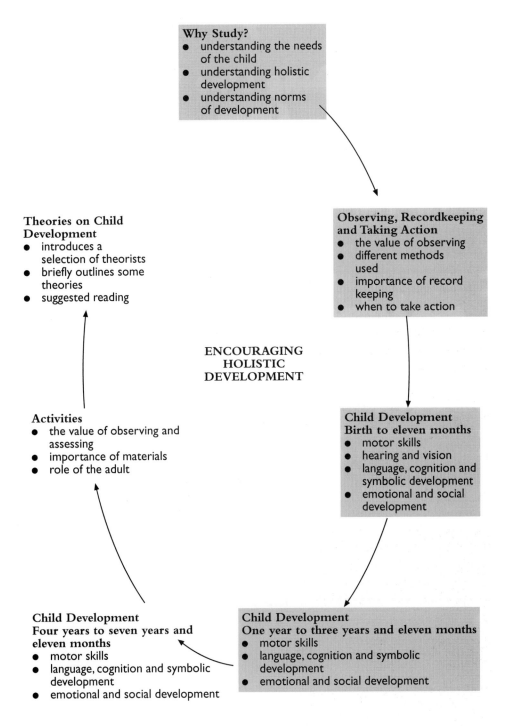

Why Study?
- understanding the needs of the child
- understanding holistic development
- understanding norms of development

Observing, Recordkeeping and Taking Action
- the value of observing
- different methods used
- importance of record keeping
- when to take action

Theories on Child Development
- introduces a selection of theorists
- briefly outlines some theories
- suggested reading

ENCOURAGING HOLISTIC DEVELOPMENT

Activities
- the value of observing and assessing
- importance of materials
- role of the adult

Child Development Birth to eleven months
- motor skills
- hearing and vision
- language, cognition and symbolic development
- emotional and social development

Child Development Four years to seven years and eleven months
- motor skills
- language, cognition and symbolic development
- emotional and social development

Child Development One year to three years and eleven months
- motor skills
- language, cognition and symbolic development
- emotional and social development

7

Approaching One Year and Over

Motor skills

Gross motor skills

▶ baby is able to sit securely for long periods
▶ if baby is walking she may intersperse this with crawling or bottom shuffling, or cruising along furniture holding on
▶ she may walk without holding on
▶ she is able to sit down from standing
▶ she can crawl upstairs

Fine motor skills

▶ baby holds on to her bottle/cup
▶ she is able to release an object from her hand deliberately and makes attempts to throw
▶ she is attempting to shuffle food onto a spoon
▶ she steers spoon to her mouth and sometimes misses or upturns spoon before it arrives
▶ she uses a pincer grasp to pick up small items

• *Helpful hint* •

Baby is rapidly becoming more mobile and needs close supervision.

OBSERVE

Observe baby's increased feeding skill.

FOCUSED OBSERVATIONS

Seek advice if baby shows little interest in attempting to feed herself.

Baby is able to feed herself with a spoon

ACTIVITY

IDEAS TO DEVELOP MOTOR SKILLS

1   provide a treasure basket containing articles of different shapes, sizes and textures. Never leave baby alone
2   provide a cardboard box (check for safety), a few bricks and safe household items and note her reactions
3   introduce a variety of food textures (one at a time)
4   encourage the use of bath toys for experimentation

Vision and hearing

Vision

▶ baby can spot small items some distance away
▶ she gives prolonged attention to activities of interest, such as siblings playing, animals or traffic

▶ her eyes follow objects which move rapidly
▶ she watches where objects fall from her hand
▶ she points with index finger
▶ she looks at pictures in books and recognises objects in pictures

Hearing

▶ baby responds promptly when her name is called
▶ she responds to simple commands, such as 'Give mummy teddy.'
▶ she imitates sounds and some words

OBSERVATION

Observe baby during a period of prolonged attention.

FOCUSED OBSERVATIONS

If baby is not responding to simple commands, or not attempting to communicate by vocalising or pointing, seek advice.

Sharing a book

ACTIVITY

IDEAS TO DEVELOP VISION AND HEARING

1 using some hand-made props, enjoy rhymes and songs with baby to encourage sound discrimination
2 provide her with a colourful toybox containing a few different types of toys, such as graduated beakers, simple construction and shapes

Language, cognition and symbolic development

▶ baby understands everyday words, for example, dinner, bath, cat
▶ she understands simple commands, such as 'Give me your bottle!'
▶ she babbles conversationally and tunefully
▶ she uses most vowels and consonants and begins to speak occasional words other than 'da-da' 'ma-ma'
▶ she draws attention to objects of interest to her by pointing, perhaps vocalising or using correct or partly correct word for the object
▶ she plays 'pretend' games and teases
▶ she understands use of familiar everyday objects

OBSERVATION

Make a checklist using simple familiar commands and tick the ones baby understands.

FOCUSED OBSERVATION

Be alert if baby does not show curiosity in her surroundings.

ACTIVITY

IDEAS TO DEVELOP LANGUAGE AND COGNITION

1 play together making pretend calls on a plastic telephone to encourage conversation
2 encourage baby to clap hands to music to encourage rhythm
3 provide an unbreakable child's mirror to encourage self concept

She is learning to use an inhaler with help from a carer

Emotional and social development

▶ baby shows fear of strangers
▶ she shows a preference for familiar carers to be near at hand
▶ she is becoming assertive
▶ most babies like some kind of comfort, for example, blanket or thumb
▶ she shows pleasure when she sees siblings and other familiar faces approaching
▶ she is beginning to assist with daily routines, such as holding out her foot for her sock to be put on
▶ she enjoys socialising at mealtimes while trying to feed herself and joins in conversation at the same time

OBSERVATION

▶ watch baby as familiar family/friends approach her after they have been out of sight
▶ observe to whom baby turns for comfort when distressed

Enjoying books

FOCUSED OBSERVATION

Note if baby does not seem to respond to the emotional and social environment around her.

ACTIVITY

IDEAS TO EXTEND EMOTIONAL AND SOCIAL DEVELOPMENT

1 ensure that baby can help with simple dressing to encourage independence
2 take baby swimming or provide water play to encourage expression of feeling
3 share books and discuss pictures

•••••••••••••••••••• *Helpful hint* ••••••••••••••••••••

Never leave baby alone with water.

8

Approaching Fifteen Months and Over

Motor skills

Gross motor skills

▶ baby sits down on the floor abruptly from standing
▶ she can sit herself on a seat at a child's height
▶ she crawls forwards upstairs and backwards downstairs with supervision
▶ she is usually able to walk on her own with a wide leg gait
▶ she can kneel, usually without holding on

Fine motor skills

▶ baby grasps crayon half way up and holds it in her palm with fingers wrapped around
▶ she may make marks and/or scribble by moving crayon backwards and forwards on the page
▶ she manipulates and looks with interest at toy cubes
▶ she can reach and put small objects in a narrow-necked container
▶ she can empty this container by turning it upside down
▶ she points to a person or object of interest to her with her index finger

---

OBSERVATION

Help to dress a child and note how a child of this age assists with the process.

FOCUSED OBSERVATION

Note any unusual degree of 'floppiness' in muscle control.

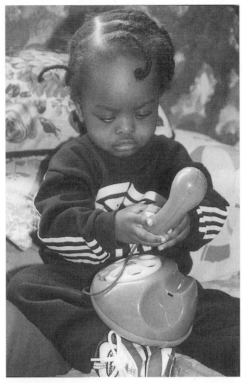

This toy provides a opportunity to develop manipulative skills

ACTIVITY

IDEAS TO DEVELOP MOTOR SKILLS

1   give baby a large crayon and plenty of paper and help her with mark making
2   provide her with two or three hats to try on and show her what she looks like in a mirror
3   provide hand-made peg people – check size for safety beforehand
4   provide push and pull toys to encourage walking and general mobility

Language, cognition and symbolic development

Language

▶ baby shows understanding of many words and commands, such as 'Give Yasmin the mug', 'Look'. Stops when commanded 'No!'
▶ she understands the names of some parts of her body
▶ she is vocalising constantly
▶ she may articulate parts of words, such as 'bis' for biscuit

▶ one word is used to mean a variety of things, for example, 'cup' may mean 'Give me the cup' or 'Look at the cup.' This is called 'holophrase'
▶ she articulates several words clearly which are associated with day-to-day happenings, such as food preparation. She may say 'Bye-bye' when she leaves

Cognition

▶ baby may copy putting one cube on top of another
▶ she pats book and looks curiously at pictures on the page
▶ she shows great interest and curiosity in her surroundings

OBSERVATION

Observe a baby linking day-to-day words with everyday happenings.

FOCUSED OBSERVATION

Note if there appear to be marked gaps in baby's understanding of language and her definition by use.

ACTIVITY

IDEAS TO DEVELOP LANGUAGE AND COGNITION

1 play a game with baby using a suitable book, for example, 'Show me the cat', 'Show me the flower' and other asking games
2 large coloured cubes and stacking toys will encourage awareness of size relationships
3 sing nursery rhymes together to encourage an awareness of repetition and memory

Emotional and social development

▶ babys' need for sleep will be individual, but daytime nap(s) are usually still needed
▶ baby cries angrily and in frustration if thwarted or misunderstood, or if needs are not met
▶ she is usually cautious of strangers
▶ she may be anxious without the presence of familiar adults or children around her
▶ she is settled in the presence of a familiar adult

▶ she is beginning to establish a sense of herself and how she can impact on other people, for example, smiling and getting a smiling response
▶ she participates noisily during mealtimes, vocalising and banging equipment
▶ she is starting to feed herself with a spoon
▶ she is keen to extend play activities and interact with children and adults
▶ she smiles in welcome to people she is familiar with

• *Helpful hint* •

Babies and young children should never be left unsupervised when eating and drinking, as they can easily choke.

OBSERVATION

Observe a baby's reaction when her most familiar carers go out of sight into another room.

FOCUSED OBSERVATION

Note if baby cries exceptionally rarely, particularly when she might be angry or frustrated.

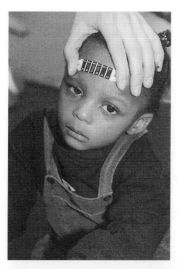

He needs comfort and reassurance from a familiar carer when feeling unwell

ACTIVITY

IDEAS TO EXTEND EMOTIONAL AND SOCIAL DEVELOPMENT

1 make a simple feely box and try it out with baby guessing what is inside
2 provide play equipment for imaginative cooking activity. Check for possible allergies and cultural requirements concerning food and its preparation

9

Approaching Eighteen Months and Over

Motor skills

Gross motor skills

▶ walking confidently, now she can stop when she wishes without falling over and she can even walk backwards. She runs cautiously

▶ she enjoys walking around carrying her favourite toys

▶ she bends down without falling over and enjoys success at pulling and pushing large toys

▶ she likes to climb and can be seen to climb forwards into a chair and then turn a round to sit

▶ she enjoys push and pull toys

Fine motor skills

▶ she will hold a pencil in her palm, or she may start to use her thumb and first two fingers in a primitive tripod grasp

▶ she enjoys making dots and moving the pencil horizontally or vertically along a piece of paper. She may begin to show a preference for using one hand in particular

▶ when she uses a paintbrush, she uses her whole arm to make strokes and will probably move the brush from hand to hand

▶ when picking up small objects she uses a pincer grasp

Bowel and bladder control

▶ she will usually go through a three-stage process: first, she will notice she has passed urine or a stool after it has happened; later on she notices while it is happening; and eventually she will react before it happens but without much time to spare

She enjoys carrying her favourite toys around

OBSERVATION

Observe an eighteen-month-old drawing. Note her grip of the pencil/crayon and whether she shows a preference for one hand.

FOCUSED OBSERVATION

If a child is unable to locate and pick up small objects and identify them, she may have a visual difficulty.

ACTIVITY

IDEAS TO DEVELOP MOTOR SKILLS

1   provide a large crayon and a large piece of paper. Keep the drawing she makes so that you can compare development in drawing in six months' time
2   provide a bag and place some of her toys inside
3   provide a soft ball and encourage throwing and catching
4   provide a large box converted into a Posting Box. Give her some 'letters' (old envelopes) to post

Language, cognition and symbolic development

Language and symbolic development

▶ she likes to repeat words she has heard and jabbers continually
▶ you are likely to hear her say between twenty and fifty recognisable words. Two words may be put together, for example, 'Dog come'. This is called 'telegraphese'
▶ she may echo the last spoken words of an adult. This is called 'echolalia'
▶ she may use pivot words (words which have a fixed position in the child's speech), for example, 'Cat gone', 'More milk', 'Dad gone'
▶ she should be able to respond to simple instructions, such as 'Give it to me'
▶ she likes to join in nursery rhymes and songs

Cognition and symbolic development

▶ curiosity and determination are strong features at this age and she is beginning to understand where things, for example, toys, belong
▶ she enjoys picture books and she sometimes names boldly printed objects
▶ placing objects in and out of containers is great fun and she will be experiencing 'size' and 'shape' and spatial relationships
▶ she is able to concentrate on one chosen activity at a time but will ignore everything else (single-channelled attention)

OBSERVATION

Observe an eighteen-month-old sharing a book with an adult. Note her interest in the pictures and any language she uses.

FOCUSED OBSERVATION

Some babies show exceptional ability in their comprehension and verbal responses. If this continues, advice should be sought.

▶ expert advice should be sought if she does not appear to respond to simple instructions and shows little interest in verbal communication

She is beginning to recognise objects in books

ACTIVITY

IDEAS TO DEVELOP LANGUAGE AND COGNITION

1   make a book out of cardboard and stick in photographs of objects
    she uses daily (or bold pictures from a magazine). Share this book with
    her
2   go for a walk and stop, look at and talk about things you see

Emotional and social development

▶ strong emotions can lead to tantrums but an increase in language can
   help with these frustrations, and appropriate play activities also channel
   these emotions. She is becoming increasingly independent and the
   word 'no' can evoke a strong reaction, but she will still respond well to
   distraction!

▶ she plays alone (solo play) and likes to be in the company of a familiar
   carer, often following carer around

▶ she shows intense curiosity and may imitate others during her play

▶ she enjoys trying to feed herself and holding a cup at meal times

▶ dressing herself is still fairly difficult but she may like to help undress herself, demonstrating her emerging independence

▶ she is trying to establish herself as a member of a social group and is beginning to understand the dynamics

---

OBSERVATION

Over a period of two hours note down the range of emotions she displays, then think of suitable activities which would best help her channel any negative emotions shown. The triggers for these emotions may be hunger, tiredness, discomfort or the onset of illness.

FOCUSED OBSERVATION

Be alert to baby if she seems excessively passive and lacking in curiosity.

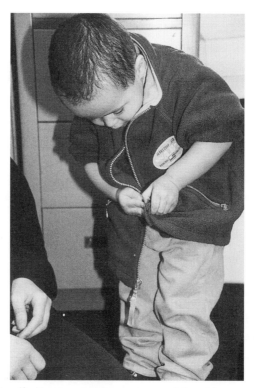

He will learn to dress himself with support and encouragement from his carer

ACTIVITY

IDEAS TO EXTEND EMOTIONAL AND SOCIAL DEVELOPMENT

1 provide ride-on toys to build up balance skills
2 provide water play. Introduce wide-neck bottles for pouring and filling to encourage an awareness of investigative learning and an awareness of cause and effect
3 provide first jigsaws to encourage her to make connections

•••••••••••••••••••••••• *Helpful hint* ••••••••••••••••••••••••

Never leave a child on her own with water – not even for a moment!

10

Approaching Two Years and Over

Motor skills

Gross motor skills

▶ she can run safely and stop smoothly when she wishes
▶ when walking up and down stairs with supervision she uses two feet to a step
▶ playing ball is greatly enjoyed and she can throw a ball over hand but cannot catch it
▶ she attempts to kick a ball but usually walks into it
▶ she pushes and pulls large toys with wheels
▶ she is unable to peddle but enjoys sitting on a tricycle and propels herself along with her feet

Fine motor skills

▶ a pincer grip is used to pick up tiny objects and she may be able to unscrew things
▶ she can build a tower of six or seven bricks
▶ her preferred hand is used for most things and when she picks up a crayon she usually uses her thumb and two fingers
▶ she experiments with circular scribbles as well as 'to and fro' scribbles and dots
▶ she can copy a vertical line and sometimes a 'V' shape
▶ she has increased skill at eating and drinking, for example scooping with a spoon and drinking from a cup with fewer spills

---

OBSERVATION

Observe a two-year-old for ten minutes during outdoor play and note which hand she prefers to use and how long she plays with any play equipment.

FOCUSED OBSERVATION

A partially sighted child may need extra encouragement in carrying out an activity, which may need to be modified.

Outdoor equipment provides opportunities for the development of fine and gross motor skills

ACTIVITY

IDEAS TO DEVELOP MOTOR SKILLS

1 provide hammer and peg toys do develop coordination
2 ball play to develop hand–eye coordination
3 large construction play
4 matching and sorting games

Language, cognition and symbolic development

Language and symbolic development

▶ she can understand a vast number of words and can probably use about sixty words in an appropriate context and will be linking two words or more together
▶ at this stage many sounds are said in an immature way

▶ around this time you will hear her overextend the use of a word, for example, all animals with four legs are 'cats'

▶ sometimes she likes to repeat what someone says over and over again, for example, 'light on, light on' and will point and use gestures to find out what objects and people are called

▶ when she talks about herself she usually uses her name

▶ while playing you will hear her talking to herself, apparently telling herself what to do!

▶ around this time she will begin to use plurals, past tense and auxiliary verbs

Cognition and symbolic development

▶ she likes to look at photographs of familiar people and may recognise herself

▶ when she is looking at books she may point out particular details or search for favourite characters and is particularly interested in the names of people and objects

▶ she will laugh at the unexpected and find it very funny if you call a cat a cow!

▶ around this time she may begin to anticipate the consequences of her own actions and those of others, for example, something falling over

▶ children at this age usually start to draw symbolically – she may produce scribbles and decide later what it represents, but rarely tries to draw what she sees

▶ she paints with a 'scrubbing' action, often one colour on top of another, and sometimes digs holes in the paper. She is indiscriminate about where the paint actually goes and is unconcerned about end product

---

OBSERVATION

Over a period of one hour listen to all the vocabulary she uses. How many *different* words did she use? Note the words she is putting together.

FOCUSED OBSERVATION

Seek advice if she shows little interest in verbal communication or if she continues to echo most of what is said to her.

ACTIVITY

IDEAS TO DEVELOP LANGUAGE AND COGNITION

1   use tapes of nursery rhymes and provide a tambourine for her to play
     (a home-made one would be just as much fun)
2   sing nursery rhymes, allowing her to join in. Choose some with repeated
     words and lines and use soft toy props, such as Humpty Dumpty
3   describe the colour of items you talk about

Emotional and social development

▶ she is beginning to express how she feels
▶ tantrums can occur when she feels unable to express herself or
   frustrated
▶ sometimes she is stable and confident and at other times dependent
   and clingy
▶ she can manage simple dressing

Close contact can help confidence

▶ she can pull pants down when being taken to the toilet or potty but needs help pulling them up

▶ she engages in 'solo play' and you may find that she watches other children for long periods (spectator play)

OBSERVATION

Observe a two-year-old in a new situation with other children and note how long she spends just looking at and watching then.

FOCUSED OBSERVATION

Seek advice if child always actively resists physical comfort.

ACTIVITY

IDEAS TO EXTEND EMOTIONAL AND SOCIAL DEVELOPMENT

1 provide resources for role play, for example, hats, gloves, loose clothing, to encourage an understanding of other roles

2 soft playing clay is useful for experimentation and pummelling to express feelings.

· · · · · · · · · · · · · · · · · · · *Helpful hints* ·

▶ high-heeled shoes can be dangerous to young children. Care must always be taken when choosing resources for role play

▶ use velcro on fastenings to aid independence

11

Approaching Two-and-a-Half Years and Over

Motor skills

Gross motor skills

▶ she can stand on tiptoe and confidently pushes and pulls large toys, but steering can sometimes be a problem
▶ when she kicks a ball she is likely to walk into it
▶ stairs are negotiated by placing two feet on every step as she holds on to the rail
▶ pedals on a tricycle are usually avoided and she effects movement by pushing it along with her feet
▶ great energy is displayed as she experiments with the limitations of her body

Fine motor skills

▶ around this time you will find that she can build a tower of seven or more blocks
▶ she usually uses her preferred hand and an improved tripod grasp when using a pencil and a fine pincer grip is in evidence when she picks up small objects
▶ she might imitate horizontal lines
▶ she may start to name her scribbles as particular things

OBSERVATION

Play a game of 'Follow the Leader' and note whether she can

a stand on tiptoe
b put on a hat
c kick a ball.

Exploring using fine motor skills

FOCUSED OBSERVATION

Seek advice if you have noticed poor co-ordination and little
development of spatial awareness.

ACTIVITY

IDEAS TO DEVELOP MOTOR SKILLS

1   provide sorting games for fine and gross activities
2   take her on an outing to a children's play area to experience outdoor
    equipment
3   provide pans, bowls and wooden spoons

Language, cognition and symbolic development

Language and symbolic development

- ▶ egocentric speech is present in play
- ▶ around this time she will be heard to ask 'What?', 'When?' and 'Who?' with increasing frequency!
- ▶ she will be using action words such as 'go' and 'out'
- ▶ she is beginning to use simple descriptions when talking about events
- ▶ she may stutter slightly when very excited or anxious to get a point across
- ▶ her speech concerns the present – what is happening now – and she may find it hard to express things that have happened in the past
- ▶ she is beginning to use plurals and pronouns and can produce two hundred or more recognisable words.

Cognition and symbolic development

- ▶ she can follow simple stories and will especially enjoy any repetition
- ▶ she knows her full name
- ▶ she can demonstrate her knowledge of parts of the body, for example, knees, toes and elbows
- ▶ she shows great curiosity in her environment and her drive to learn is evident in her play
- ▶ her thinking is tied to what can be seen, as she cannot yet consider abstract concepts
- ▶ internal thought is indicated by the fact that she can make one thing stand for another in simple role play, for example, a broom could be a horse.
- ▶ concentration can be maintained for up to fifteen minutes in an activity which is interesting and absorbing and an adult can guide her attention from one task to another provided there are no distractions

---

OBSERVATION

Tape a two-and-a-half-year-old playing with small world playthings. Listen back to the tape and note down all the words she uses which are plurals and any pronouns.

Practising filling and emptying vessels in water play

FOCUSED OBSERVATION

Expert advice should be sought if her speech is mostly not understandable and she is not able to carry out short commands, such as 'Give teddy a cuddle'.

ACTIVITY

IDEAS TO DEVELOP LANGUAGE AND COGNITION

1   provide simple musical instruments and listen to tapes of different musical traditions to encourage an understanding of a range of communication skills
2   watch a favourite video together and afterwards talk about it together
3   make a simple mask together, talk about how you are making it and play a pretend game afterwards
4   a communication method such as makaton may be introduced to children who have communication difficulties

Emotional and social development

▶ she sees most things from her point of view (egocentric), behaving impulsively, wanting everything and anything she sees. She wants to try out everything!

▶ she has very strong outbursts in response to frustration

▶ she needs calm reassurance when experiencing irrational fears

▶ although she is gaining in confidence she can still swing very quickly from 'positive' to 'negative' behaviour

▶ sometimes she likes to be helpful to others but only if this doesn't conflict with her own wishes!

▶ her sense of self-identity is developing

OBSERVATION

Watch a two-and-a-half-year-old playing near other children. Do you think she is nearly ready to join in their play?

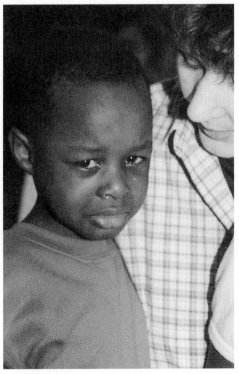

Children need calm reassurance from their carer

FOCUSED OBSERVATION

Seek advice if she shows little interest or curiosity in near opportunities and her surroundings.

ACTIVITY

IDEAS TO EXTEND EMOTIONAL AND SOCIAL DEVELOPMENT

1   sand play is useful to express feelings
2   dancing and jumping to music with other children encourages self-expression
3   provide large apparatus for climbing into and up and down, including low ramps and steps
4   skittles play can improve coordination skills, but also give opportunities to explore success, disappointment, perseverence and turn-taking

• *Helpful hint* •

▶   provide a hat as this will keep sand out of her hair

12

Approaching Three Years and Over

Motor skills

Gross motor skills

▶ for a short while she can stand and walk on tiptoe
▶ around this age you will find that she can walk backwards and sideways and can stand on one foot
▶ she is learning to run with more confidence
▶ she climbs stairs one foot to a step and descends two feet to a step
▶ she enjoys jumping off a low step
▶ spatial awareness is well developed and you will see her manoeuvre herself and her toys around objects
▶ you might find that around this time she can use pedals on a tricycle
▶ now she can throw a ball overhead and can catch a ball with arms outstretched
▶ she can kick a ball using her whole body to generate a powerful kick

Fine motor skills

▶ children of this age enjoy building towers and she can now build tall towers using nine or ten bricks
▶ she can use a dynamic tripod (thumb and first two fingers)
▶ she holds a pencil with developing control
▶ she might copy a circle and is beginning to develop some understanding of letter shapes
▶ she uses a paintbrush, making rhythmical strokes
▶ she uses scissors mostly to good effect
▶ she is able to take part in simple craft activities and daily tasks, for example, placing stamps on envelopes

OBSERVATION

With permission, video a three-year-old playing on large play equipment outdoors for ten minutes. (If a video camera is not available,

He shows increasing ability in simple cutting tasks

please just observe and record.) Using a column for gross motor skills and a column for fine motor skills, note down all the physical skills she demonstrates during this play.

FOCUSED OBSERVATION

Ask for further guidance if she frequently falls over.

ACTIVITY

IDEAS TO DEVELOP MOTOR SKILLS

The following list of activities provides ideas for promoting fine and gross motor skills:

1 threading toys
2 crayons, large and small, and non-toxic felt tip pens
3 safe scissors, paper and pencils
4 large brushes, paper and paint
5 craft activities associated with festivals and seasons
6 building blocks and puzzles
7 tricycles
8 balls – for catching and throwing
9 trucks to pull and push
10 sand and water play with sieves, different vessels, water wheels, for example
11 large building blocks
12 large foam balls

Language, cognition and symbolic development

Language and symbolic development

▶ she will develop good listening skills if she is listened to patiently and with genuine interest

▶ sentence structure can be immature and pronunciation can be infantile at this age

▶ she possesses a large vocabulary, perhaps approaching several hundred words

▶ she is starting to link three or four words together in a sentence, but may miss out small words like 'and' 'the' and 'is'

▶ she is trying to use language in a variety of ways, for example, making requests, telling about things, and taking turns in conversation

▶ sometimes she will ask for help and may enjoy telling everyone what to do!

▶ she talks to herself while playing and is beginning to communicate about past events as well as present

▶ you may hear her make up words and she will experiment with new sounds

▶ she enjoys laughing at jokes she understands

▶ she may stop and start within a sentence, apparently struggling for the right word

▶ she will be starting to use, action words, such as 'run' and 'eat', and describing words, such as 'small', 'clean' and 'happy'

▶ she enjoys communicating through music using singing, rhymes and musical instruments

▶ children who have the opportunity may be becoming fluent in more than one language

Cognition and symbolic development

▶ she can match two or three primary colours with relevant objects but blue and green are often confused

▶ three-year-olds often draw 'tadpole' people which eventually progress to include legs and then arms

▶ 'patch' painting emerges and she often knows what she is painting. She concentrates well and seems more concerned about the finished product but this is not always recognisable to the adult

▶ there is now some appreciation of the difference between the present and the past

- ▶ she can begin to sort objects into simple categories
- ▶ she may enjoy counting numbers up to ten but understanding of one number, one object comes later
- ▶ she is fascinated by cause and effect and will spend time asking 'Why?' and wondering about things
- ▶ she is beginning to understand about seasonal differences in the weather
- ▶ she may show an interest in learning new skills, for example, how to operate simple computer games
- ▶ at times she confuses fact and fiction in stories and likes to relate events in stories to events in her own life
- ▶ thinking back about past events is easier for her now
- ▶ songs and rhymes are remembered and repeated with reasonable accuracy
- ▶ there are signs that she is beginning to control her attention, choosing to stop an activity and return to the task without much difficulty

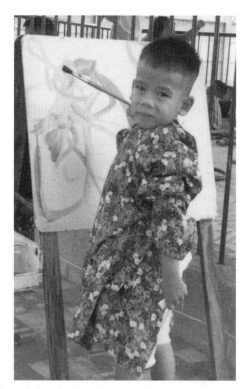

Painting and drawing skills are being developed

OBSERVATION

Plan and prepare a simple sorting activity, such as sorting out her toy cars and blocks and placing them into their own containers. (She may need help.) Note down her interest and understanding of this activity.

FOCUSED OBSERVATIONS

Seek advice if your observations show that:

a she is consistently using a restricted number of words

b she is not putting two or three words together

c she is not using a wide range of sounds and many people find her difficult to understand

d she is slow in following instructions and needs them to be repeated

ACTIVITY

IDEAS TO DEVELOP LANGUAGE AND COGNITION

The following list of activities provide ideas for promoting language, cognition and symbolic understanding:

1 stencils, templates and tracing equipment

2 matching and sorting games using toy cars, toy animals

3 simple computer games

4 musical instruments with examples from different cultures, such as glockenspiel

5 listening, responding and questioning games

6 videos showing instruments and their sounds

7 books – self-made books demonstrating examples from her own interests, for example, recalling a walk in the park when she used a magnifying glass or binoculars

8 weather chart, to discuss the different types of weather

9 rubbings from trees, buildings, coins, for discussion of textures, shape, etc.

Emotional and social development

▶ irrational fears can still be evident and very real to her and she may need support to cope in new or different situations

▶ she is keen to do things unaided – 'I do it myself'

▶ she is learning to cope with hurtful remarks or actions which may sometimes occur in her relationships

▶ she is beginning to show that she can think about things from somebody else's perspective

▶ her expanding vocabulary permits her to express her feelings verbally
▶ her play shows great imagination and provides an outlet for her emotions
▶ her manner may be more contented, friendly and helpful
▶ she enjoys helping and seeks adult approval, for example, helping to tidy up
▶ friendships may be important to her and some strong attachments may be made to individual children
▶ care for younger children and animals may be shown
▶ she is becoming aware of differences between people, for example, different sexes, ethnic and cultural identities
▶ associative play is now present as she is truly beginning to interact with other children. Solo play continues
▶ with encouragement she can take turns when playing

Handpainting offers an ideal opportunity to experience and experiment with paint

OBSERVATION

Observe a three-year-old in a role play situation. Write down what is happening using the present tense and then analyse the play. Did the child need many props to support this play? What 'role' was she playing?

FOCUSED OBSERVATION

Seek advice if she shows no interest in beginning to interact with other children.

ACTIVITY

IDEAS TO EXTEND EMOTIONAL AND SOCIAL DEVELOPMENT

The following list provides suggestions for activities for promoting social and emotional development:

1   role play situations, in the form of hairdressers (provide the range of pretend conditioning treatment and equipment for all hair types), café, Post Office, fire station, home area (supply a range of resources which reflect a multicultural society, for example, cooking utensils and different types of pretend food, such as a variety of vegetables, different types of bread)
2   role play clothes (hats, turbans, trousers, saris). Clothes should be easy for children with disabilities to put on. Avoid shoes with high heels
3   outings for example, to the zoo, farm, to the park
4   fuzzy felts
5   hand and foot prints, for comparison of shape and size with other children
6   play garage and cars

Summary of Part 3

▶ watchful, constant supervision is essential as she experiments with her physical capabilities
▶ enthusiastic adults who celebrate the child's achievements will provide a good basis from which the child can try out new skills and ideas
▶ a significant growth in language skills opens up new possibilities.

Part 4
Child Development

Aims

To help you to understand:

▶ Literacy and numeracy development
▶ the increasing awareness of self and others
▶ the development of an awareness of understanding cause and effect.

Key issues:

▶ Literacy and numeracy development. It is important that early years workers create an environment where speaking and listening skills are encouraged. A wide range of reading and writing materials need to be available and bilingual children need books which provide them with the opportunity to read in both languages.
▶ She is developing an increasing awareness of self and others.
▶ She is developing an awareness of understanding cause and effect.

Carer plays a vital role in helping children develop hand/eye co-ordination

Why Study?
- understanding the needs of the child
- understanding holistic development
- understanding norms of development

Observing, Recordkeeping and Taking Action
- the value of observing
- different methods used
- importance of record keeping
- when to take action

Theories on Child Development
- introduces a selection of theorists
- briefly outlines some theories
- suggested reading

ENCOURAGING HOLISTIC DEVELOPMENT

Activities
- the value of observing and assessing
- importance of materials
- role of the adult

Child Development Birth to eleven months
- motor skills
- hearing and vision
- language, cognition and symbolic development
- emotional and social development

Child Development Four years to seven years and eleven months
- motor skills
- language, cognition and symbolic development
- emotional and social development

Child Development One year to three years and eleven months
- motor skills
- language, cognition and symbolic development
- emotional and social development

13

Approaching Four Years and Over

Motor skills

Gross motor skills

▶ she can stand or even run on tiptoe
▶ she runs skillfully, turning corners and stopping and starting with ease
▶ she can climb stairs confidently
▶ when riding a tricycle, she rides with skill and can make sharp turns easily
▶ she continues in her attempts to throw and catch a ball
▶ using hands and feet she can manoeuvre herself over large apparatus

Fine motor skills

▶ once she has been shown how, she is able to use six bricks to build three steps
▶ increased fine manipulative control is evident, for example, she can undo some buttons when undressing
▶ she will attempt a letter 'X' and attempt to form initial letters of her name or others', possibly also 'V', 'H' and 'O'
▶ she is able to thread smaller beads than she could when she was three
▶ she demonstrates increasing skill with pencil control, usually using preferred hand and can draw a person with arms, legs and body, and sometimes fingers appear too. Drawings are visually recognisable

---

OBSERVATION

With permission of the parent and responsible adult in the setting, take photographs of a four-year-old which demonstrate a range of gross and fine motor skills. Assess which activities might further develop these skills.

FOCUSED OBSERVATION

If she always appears to need to hold objects close to her face, she may have difficulty seeing them at a greater distance. Advice should be sought.

These children are demonstrating increased fine manipulative control

ACTIVITY

IDEAS TO DEVELOP MOTOR SKILLS

1   provide a four-year-old with paper and crayons and ask her to draw
    something she wishes to draw. Note what she says while she is drawing
    and what she tells you it is when she has finished
2   printing with paint using blocks, sponges or string to encourage
    hand–eye coordination
3   provide different materials for modeling, such as soft playing clay, or
    papier mâché to encourage representation
4   encourage construction using junk, building blocks, empty cartons
5   woodwork – under supervision
6   computer – use of mouse and paint programs
7   provide hoops, bats, bean bags and balls to extend coordination skills

Language, cognition and symbolic development

Language and symbolic development

▶ she is asking Why? When? and How? Can I have? Can I go?

▶ she can give an account of a recent experience

▶ she is able to talk about things she is going to do

▶ she can recite her full name and address almost correctly

▶ some four-year-olds are becoming fluent in two or more languages

▶ she finds jokes and play on words tremendous fun

▶ she can repeat full nursery rhymes and number rhymes or songs with few errors

▶ she might enjoy making up words

▶ absurdities make her laugh, for example, if the cat says 'Oink' or if a cat is said to have wings!

▶ she uses 'in', 'on', 'under' and understands 'who', 'whose', 'how' and 'why'

▶ she may not be able to pronounce sounds such as 'r' or 'th' and strings of sounds like 'str' (in straw) or 'scr' (in scrap) and 'sps' (in crisps)

▶ she is beginning to use language to negotiate

▶ her speech is generally grammatically correct but she tries to make grammatically irregular words fit grammatical rules, for example, 'I goed' for 'I went' or 'runned' for 'ran'

▶ she might recognise familiar words, such as her own name or brand names on packets

Cognition and symbolic development

▶ she can listen to a story, following events carefully. At times fact and fantasy are still confused

▶ with encouragement she will be learning that print has meaning and she may begin to communicate through the use of pictures, symbols or isolated letters

▶ she is beginning to understand some abstract ideas, such as fair play and right and wrong

▶ she may enjoy counting up to twenty by rote and may display an actual understanding of number up to three

▶ drawing is beginning to include more detail, for example, bodies begin to be added to heads, and hands and fingers are added to arms

▶ while she is painting, she may change her mind about the design She often provides a monologue while painting and is taking increasing satisfaction in the end product

▶ mostly she keeps on-task during a self-chosen activity and can stop what she is doing and return her attention to it without adult help

OBSERVATION

Observe a group of four-year-olds during a story-telling session and note their responses.

FOCUSED OBSERVATIONS

Some children show an unusual ability to understand complex relationships and advice should be sought about the best ways to support their understanding.

Seek advice if a child constantly repeats phrases or questions, avoids eye contact, lacks imagination or whose behaviour is consistently inappropriate.

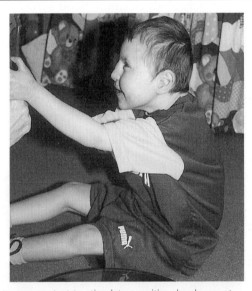

The carer provides one-to-one contact to stimulate cognitive development

ACTIVITY

IDEAS TO DEVELOP LANGUAGE AND COGNITION

1 tell and retell stories using repetitive phrases to encourage an understanding of sequencing
2 invite parents to come and share stories in the child's heritage language and allow time for the child to respond and the adults to listen
3 join a book club to gain access to a range of texts
4 make a book together – using story props made from lolly sticks and wooden spoons
5 supply a range of writing materials and paper, little cards, envelopes
6 use a computer program designed to encourage problem solving

Emotional and social development

▶ the needs of others are now considered and she may show great sensitivity

▶ she is becoming very sociable and talkative both with adults and children

▶ working out right from wrong is quite a challenge and she is watching and listening to make an attempt to understand

▶ she may boast of her accomplishments and enjoys demonstrating newly acquired skills

▶ she may show an interest in her own development – What were her first words? Which toy did she like best?

▶ she can manage self-help skills but may need some help cutting food and with personal care and hygiene

▶ she may still be at the 'associative' play stage or she may be starting to play cooperatively, sharing goals with others. Solo play continues

▶ her involvement in imaginative play will help her to cope with varying emotions. This play can be elaborate and prolonged

▶ she is beginning to share adult time/attention with others

Playing imaginatively together

Observation

Observe a four-year-old at play with others. Note what roles she adopts and are assigned.

Focused observations

A child with a learning difficulty may find self-help skills hard and the carer will need to consider different ways to enable the child to succeed, for example, the use of velcro as a fastening.

A C T I V I T Y

Ideas to extend emotional and social development

1 make a book together about her first year of life. Include photos, list of favourite foods, drawings of special people, for promoting a sense of identity
2 feely box/textures/what does the child like/dislike?
3 role play. Provide a range of simple dressing-up resources which reflect different cultures. Avoid shoes with high heels. This helps the child explore social diversity
4 involve child in caring for pets to develop a sense of responsibility

14

Approaching Five Years and Over

Motor skills

Gross motor skills

▶ she may enjoy throwing a ball but will probably still catch using her whole arm
▶ she plays ball games with good coordination and can dance to music, moving rhythmically
▶ activities such as climbing and swinging also demonstrate this increasing coordination and balance
▶ she enjoys riding a two-wheeled bike but usually needs stabilisers
▶ she can dress without much supervision; she may still find tying laces difficult

Fine motor skills

▶ she usually shows a right- or left-hand preference
▶ she may copy more characters, for example, 'V', 'T', 'H', 'O','X', 'I', 'A', 'C', 'U', 'Y'

OBSERVATION

With permission, take a series of photographs of a five-year-old which clearly demonstrate the child's developing gross motor skills, for example, climbing, dancing or swinging

FOCUSED OBSERVATION

▶ special note needs to be taken of any clear evidence of poor hand/eye coordination and if she moves her head rather than eye when looking at pictures or stories
▶ children with visual difficulties may avoid games and activities which depend upon good vision and coordination, such as ball games

She may show a right-or left-hand preference when holding a pencil

---

ACTIVITY

IDEAS TO DEVELOP MOTOR SKILLS

1 using glue stick and manipulating small size materials to form small size mozaics or collage patterns
2 ball games – throwing a ball/bean bag into a box
3 manipulating large and small construction materials to form stable and extensive structures

---

Language, cognition and symbolic development

Language and symbolic development

▶ increased skills enable her to engage in conversations with adults and children and show she understands the different purposes of words

▶ 'what does that mean?' is a question she will often ask about abstract words

▶ 'what if?' questions demonstrate her understanding of past, present and future

▶ she is able to pronounce most of the sounds of her heritage language

▶ she is able to use both the family accent and that of the locality

▶ she loves to tell and make up jokes and riddles

▶ drawings are showing good detail, for example, a house may have windows, a door, a roof and a chimney. She has reached the 'realism' stage in her drawings, clearly representing what is seen. Usually she has a clear idea of what she wishes to paint and rarely deviates from the idea. She might become frustrated if she finds that she cannot portray the ideas. Colours are chosen with deliberation

Cognitive and symbolic development

▶ she can usually match many colours

▶ her sense of time is developing and she is beginning to realise that the clock time has a relationship to the daily routine of events

▶ comprehension of events/stories can often be seen through watching her acting out scenes, sometimes with others, sometimes on her own

▶ if she has a special interest, for example plants, she may show an in-depth knowledge

▶ she is beginning to show an increasing interest in reading and writing

▶ she may be able to retell a favourite story while appropriately turning the pages of the book and will use picture cues

▶ she may recognise not only her own name but that of others and may also demonstrate a knowledge of phonics – some initial sounds

▶ she may be able to write some letter shapes in response to speech sounds and letter names – describing her drawing or making an attempt at writing her name

▶ single-channelled attention is fading as she can now listen to an adult's instruction without stopping what she is doing

---

OBSERVATION

Prepare some simple puppets and create a basic theatre. Ask two five-year-olds to make up a short play and tell them you will be their
· audience when they are ready. Note down the use of expression in their voices, the main plot and their enjoyment of the play!

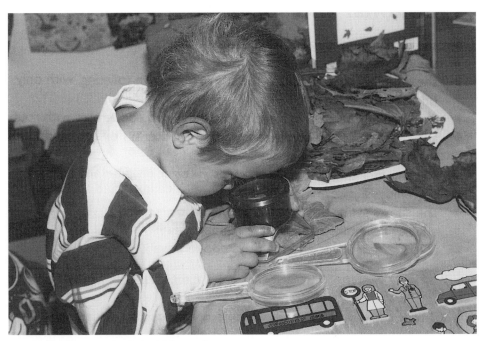

Curiosity and investigation help children to learn

FOCUSED OBSERVATION

▶ if she has difficulty in asking and answering questions and there is a marked lack of fluency, then speech and language help and advice should be sought

▶ it may be necessary to assess a child for possible colour blindness if she continues to be confused about colours

ACTIVITY

IDEAS TO DEVELOP LANGUAGE AND COGNITION

1 provide a range of reference books, and both fiction and non-fiction stories to encourage an awareness of a range of texts
2 provide a variety of writing equipment to encourage spontaneous attempts at communication
3 provide colouring and measuring equipment to encourage mathematical understanding
4 provide sprouting seeds and pips to grow to encourage an awareness of how elements effect growth

Emotional and social development

▶ she can be generous and kind towards others
▶ she enjoys one-to-one relationships
▶ she is usually reliable during the day for her own toileting, with only occasional accidents
▶ she generally behaves in a more stable way and cooperates with routine
▶ she can feed herself competently using the utensils or her hands, whichever is usual in her family
▶ she shows a caring attitude towards younger children and animals
▶ she enjoys a joke
▶ she shows sympathy towards friends who are hurt
▶ she can now take straightforward messages
▶ solo play continues and she plays cooperatively

OBSERVATION

Choose a five-year-old with whom you have contact during the day. Briefly record your conversations with this child. At the end of the day use the following two headings to divide your responses to the child:

Positive responses   Negative responses

Evaluate your findings and see whether you need to be more encouraging in your responses.

A child enjoying the company of his pet

FOCUSED OBSERVATION

By this age children who are not toilet-trained by day or night and do not have any identifiable disability will require further help and advice.

ACTIVITY

IDEAS TO EXTEND EMOTIONAL AND SOCIAL DEVELOPMENT

1   talk about people who help us, such as fire fighters. Perhaps make a book together and plan a visit to the fire station
2   she can be entrusted with some simple tasks, for example washing up, carrying shopping, planting seeds
3   make books together about 'things we eat' or 'things beginning with the same letter' as the beginning of the child's name

15

Approaching Six Years and Over

Motor skills

Gross motor skills

▶ she is agile and her strength is well developed. She appears to be constantly 'on the go'. She can make a vertical jump of about ten centimetres and land with confidence
▶ she jumps off appropriate school apparatus with confidence
▶ she can kick a football three-to-six metres and make a running jump of approximately one hundred centimetres
▶ she is able to learn some dance sequences and movement is well coordinated
▶ she can ride a two-wheeled bike, usually using stabilisers
▶ general muscle coordination and balance is now well developed

Fine motor skills

▶ around this time you will see that she can build a virtually straight tower
▶ pencil control is well developed as she is now able to grasp and adjust the pencil and her hold is similar to that of an adult
▶ she may be familiar with different written language formations. For example, her heritage language may have different characters and/or be written from right to left

---

OBSERVATION

Observe a six-year-old involved in outdoor play. Write down as much as you can about her gross and fine motor control, her general coordination and agility.

FOCUSED OBSERVATION

Advice needs to be sought if she has general poor gross and fine motor control, and obvious difficulty in dressing and undressing.

Improved muscle co-ordination enables her to kick a football some distance

ACTIVITY

IDEAS TO DEVELOP MOTOR SKILLS

1 provide hoops, bean-bags, balls, bats, skipping ropes and introduce team games and games with rules
2 provide cooking activities (under supervision) and use different types of dough, pastry, pasta, poppadom, naan, dumplings
3 use papier mâché to make crafts and toys for displays and festivals

Language, cognition and symbolic development

Language and symbolic development

▶ she understands the rules of turn-taking in conversation
▶ continual questioning is slackening
▶ she uses about four to seven words to make accurate sentences using 'could' and 'would'

▶ she loves to talk about everything and anything, telling and making up jokes

▶ she can answer the phone in quite a mature manner and communicates clearly

▶ although she may be able to pronounce most of the sounds of her language, she may have difficulty with 'L', 'V', 'F' and 'S' in the English language

Cognition and symbolic development

▶ her mind is very active and decisions are not made as quickly as before, as she is capable of weighing up possibilities

▶ it is easier for her to follow three-part instructions, for example, 'Go to the bedroom and bring the crayons for your friends'

▶ concepts of matter, for example, length, measurement, distance, area, time, volume, capacity and weight, are developing

▶ mostly, she can distinguish between what is fact and fantasy

▶ with encouragement she will show an increasing interest in a range of written text and begin to use a number of strategies to decode text including interpreting illustrations, effective use of phonics and the beginning of the ability to predict and self-correct

▶ she draws people using detail. She may, for example, include eyelashes, eyebrows, buttons and zips on clothes. Attempts might be made to draw a house showing that she understands that there is more than one side to a house

▶ with encouragement she will begin to produce short pieces of writing and to spell a range of simple words

▶ she has fully integrated attention – she is able to watch, listen and carry out simple things at the same time

---

OBSERVATION

Set up a simple magnetic experiment and observe her evaluating which items attract and repel.

FOCUSED OBSERVATION

Be alert if she appears to be unable to follow simple instructions, for example, 'Go and get your lunch box and wait by the door.'

An interested adult encourages the development of literacy

ACTIVITY

IDEAS TO DEVELOP LANGUAGE AND COGNITION

1   trip to the library – both children's fiction and non-fiction sections
2   outings to museums, art exhibitions, observatory, airport to provide an understanding of the wider world
3   items such as magnets, microscopes, minibeasts, globe and telescope to assist in studying the natural world
4   computer programs to support any of the above activities
5   child's electronic keyboard to encourage skills of composition and creativity

Emotional and social development

▶ she is showing quite clearly that she is able to 'decentre', considering the wishes of others
▶ she might be distressed if her friendships are disrupted by disagreement

• *Helpful hint* •

Ensure children do not attempt to look at bright lights or the sun through a telescope

▶ she might wish to take some responsibility for helping younger children, particularly in play situations

▶ she may be able to describe quite clearly how she feels, for example, sadness at a particular situation or excitement about a forthcoming event

▶ at this stage of development she may be very good at evaluating her own skills, for example, good at running/not so good at running, good at reading/not so good at reading

▶ she is also greatly influenced by her growing ability to interpret what others think/feel about her

▶ behaviour is now reasonably controlled and appropriate in a variety of social situations

▶ cooperative games are now enjoyed as she can play cooperatively with others

▶ during role play she may assign roles to others and together they may predict what will happen in their pretend play

---

OBSERVATION

Observe a group of six-year-olds involved in fantasy play. Note whether they decide at the outset how the play will progress and the roles each will play, or whether the play evolves without any planning.

Swinging is an exciting and comforting experience

Focused observation

Be alert if she does not seem able to show emotions such as happiness and sadness.

ACTIVITY

Ideas to extend emotional and social development

1 make a book with her about things she is good at doing, such as swimming, catching a ball, kicking a ball to help her celebrate her strengths
2 introduce non-competitive games to encourage cooperation
3 make scrap books of topics of their interest to encourage self-esteem
4 collecting objects of interest, for use when making models or displays

16

Approaching Seven Years and Over

Motor skills

Gross motor skills

▶ her movements are precise and she may be able to walk along a thin line with arms outstretched for balance and can hop on either leg
▶ hopping comes easily and she is able to remain well balanced
▶ she may be quite expert at riding a two-wheeled bicycle without aid
▶ she can negotiate climbing apparatus with good skill and may play games and run and jump around energetically outside
▶ she can jump off low apparatus at school and will practise skills many times in order to perfect the skill
▶ her skill at catching a ball is improved
▶ given an opportunity she may wish to try her skills out in a variety of sporting activities, for example, trampolining, swimming and roller skating
▶ she may be able to control her speed when running and swerve to avoid collision, and show good spatial awareness

Fine motor skills

▶ she can build tall, straight towers using bricks
▶ sewing is mastered around this age but a large needle is necessary
▶ her drawings and paintings will show an increased desire for detail and will include clothing and sometimes originality in the stance of a person

---

OBSERVATION

Ask her to draw her home and note how she arranges the detail.

FOCUSED OBSERVATION

Children with visual difficulties will need help in developing confidence in the other four senses.

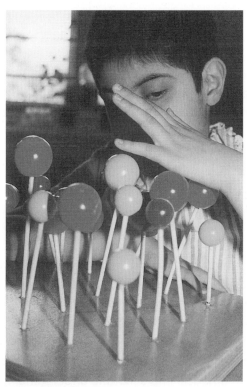

This child is gaining confidence by means of visual stimulation

ACTIVITY

IDEAS TO DEVELOP MOTOR SKILLS

The following list provides ideas for strengthening gross and fine motor skill:

1   obstacle games
2   drawing using a variety of materials, such as charcoal, wax, paint, *découpage* (paper cut-outs)
3   sewing
4   maintaining a garden area
5   metal detector
6   swings, stepping stones, old tyre to help with coordination and balance

Language, cognition and symbolic development

Language and symbolic development

▶   if she speaks more than one language, the degree of fluency in each will vary

▶ jokes can now be complex – humour hinges on ambiguity, for example, she finds it funny if words sound alike but have different meanings

▶ with encouragement she can express her emotions in words

▶ she may have achieved mastery of most regularities and exceptions in language – plurals and past tenses – but can sometimes be heard to say such things as, 'I brang the bag home'

Cognition and symbolic development

▶ she will show great pride in her accomplishments

▶ she may be interested in design and working models

▶ the challenge of experimenting and manipulating new material is enjoyed at this age

▶ her interest and skills in Information Technology may be developing rapidly

▶ she may ask questions about cause and effect, such as boiling water and evaporation

▶ she expresses 'awe and wonder' and interest in life and death issues

▶ around this time she will be extending her understanding of earlier concepts of mathematical and scientific understanding, for example, the way an oval ball rolls in comparison to a round ball

▶ she is beginning to tell the time

▶ she is beginning to do simple calculations in her head

▶ she can manage small amounts of money

▶ around this time she is beginning to understand about people's intentions

▶ drawings may indicate increasing detail of 'insides' of objects and personal style might develop and may be very original

▶ her interest in talking, listening, writing and reading are usually well underway and she will be listening attentively to stories and poems, participating by speaking in groups and using picture, context and phonic cues in reading

▶ she produces short pieces of writing independently and is beginning to apply her knowledge of patterns in spelling when attempting to spell a wider range of words (common prefixes and suffixes)

OBSERVATION

Provide two seven-year-olds with junk material and set the task of designing a working model. Ask them to draw their plans first. Take particular note of their ability to critically evaluate the finished item.

Information technology provides a source of entertainment and learning

---

FOCUSED OBSERVATION

If she has difficulty in understanding complex language and is experiencing problems relating to other children, advice should be sought.

ACTIVITY

IDEAS TO DEVELOP LANGUAGE AND COGNITION

1 involve children in a puppetry show to encourage expressive language and intonation
2 provide opportunities for composing music and poetry to encourage creativity (children with communication difficulties may benefit from using computers/communication boards, Makaton and other signing methods)
3 cause and effect experiments, for example, freezing temperatures – expansion and contraction, water mills
4 experiments with light – reflection and refraction
5 concave and convex mirrors
6 making crystals

Emotional and social development

▶ she is beginning to demonstrate a wide range of appropriate emotional responses

▶ concepts such as helpfulness, fairness and forgiveness are developing

▶ she is able to control her emotions, thus allowing her to 'hide' her feelings when she wishes

▶ friendships are very important and the peer group may be very influential

▶ she may be able to speak up for herself, for example, when she is visiting the dentist

▶ she is able to take care of animals effectively but will probably need reminding to attend to their needs on a regular basis

▶ all the basic skills needed for independence in hygiene and toileting routines are achieved

▶ as she is watching and absorbing much at this stage she may seem quieter

▶ she may be very critical about her own work

▶ play is elaborate and she will involve herself in complex cooperative play and games with rules

---

OBSERVATION

Choose a method of observing emotional and social development relevant to this age group – perhaps event- or time-sampling – and do this over the course of perhaps a week. How do you think this child is developing? Can you think of any helpful activities to develop this child's emotional and social development further?

FOCUSED OBSERVATION

Advice should be sought if she is distracted very easily, if she flits from one activity to another, and she appears overactive.

Animals help foster a caring attitude

ACTIVITY

IDEAS TO EXTEND EMOTIONAL AND SOCIAL DEVELOPMENT

The following activities will encourage children to express themselves in an acceptable way and learn about relationships:

1 clay and modelling
2 try out food–tasting experiments under supervision
3 cook for a special festival under supervision
4 set up a display of artistic work taken from a range of different cultures across the world
5 help children make a 'den'

Summary of Part 4

▶ Literacy and numeracy development-it is important that early years workers create an environment where speaking and listening skills are encouraged. A wide range of reading and writing materials need to be available and bilingual children need books which provide them with the opportunity to read in both languages.
▶ She is developing an increasing awareness of self and others.
▶ She is developing an awareness of understanding cause and effect.

Part 5

Activities and theories

Aims

▶ to understand the value of observing and assessing in order to plan for activities
▶ why it is necessary to use a range of materials
▶ the role of the adult during activities
▶ to introduce the reader to a selection of theorists
▶ to give a brief outline of some of the theories on aspects of children's development researched by well known theorists
▶ to provide the reader with a reading list should they wish to study a particular theory in depth.

Why Study?
- understanding the needs of the child
- understanding holistic development
- understanding norms of development

Observing, Recordkeeping and Taking Action
- the value of observing
- different methods used
- importance of record keeping
- when to take action

Theories on Child Development
- introduces a selection of theorists
- briefly outlines some theories
- suggested reading

ENCOURAGING HOLISTIC DEVELOPMENT

Activities
- the value of observing and assessing
- importance of materials
- role of the adult

**Child Development
Birth to eleven months**
- motor skills
- hearing and vision
- language, cognition and symbolic development
- emotional and social development

**Child Development
Four years to seven years and eleven months**
- motor skills
- language, cognition and symbolic development
- emotional and social development

**Child Development
One year to three years and eleven months**
- motor skills
- language, cognition and symbolic development
- emotional and social development

17

Activities

Aims of the chapter

To help you to understand:

▶ the value of observing and assessing in order to plan for activities.
▶ why it is necessary to use a range of materials.
▶ the role of the adult during activities.

The value of observing and assessing

Early years workers welcome practical suggestions on how to help children to develop further. An essential knowledge of child development cannot be put to good use without the knowledge of how to choose, plan and provide suitable activities. Time is well spent observing children carefully to make an assessment of their development – early years workers can suggest possible activities in their recommendations (see *How to Make Observations and Assessments*, Harding and Meldon-Smith).

Does the observation and assessment bring to light any particular need? For example, does the observation indicate that the child has difficulty concentrating, or perhaps peddling a tricycle?

Individuality

Every child develops in an individual way and activities need to be planned with the individual child in mind. We must recognise that each child has unique potential and early years workers must strive to help each child make progress towards that potential.

•••••••••••••••••••• *Helpful hints* ••••••••••••••••••••

PLANNING ACTIVITIES

Questions to be considered when planning activities:

▶ What might this activity help the child to achieve?
▶ Is the activity too easy or too difficult? Can all children in the group participate?
▶ Does the activity uphold the principles of equality of opportunity?

▶ Is the activity safe?
▶ Will the activity build on previous experience?
▶ Does the activity encourage the child to explore and investigate?
▶ Does the activity provide opportunity for the child to talk to other children and adults?

The above points may not occur all at once.

Materials to use

It is important to offer children a range of materials with which they can experiment and investigate.

Children need a range of equipment to develop their skills

The importance of giving children the opportunity to repeat skills cannot be underestimated. The child who practises the same puzzle over and over again may be wishing to affirm her skill and enjoy the success of the finished product.

Active play outside brings fresh challenges and opportunities for the child to practise gross motor skills and develop an understanding of the natural environment.

Role of the adult

To show enthusiasm: adults who engage in help and support in an enthusiastic way are very encouraging to the child who is attempting new skills.

To give attention: genuine and patient attention from an interested adult is invaluable. Cries of 'Watch me' or 'Listen to me' while they perform a new skill or use a new piece of material indicate the need for adult approval and attention. The response from adults can determine the willingness to

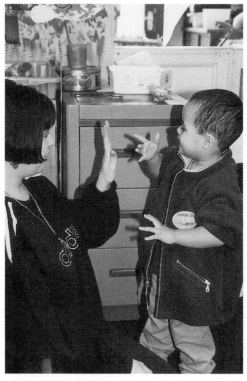

Patient reinforcement is needed when learning new concepts

have another try or move on to new skills. A smile, words of encouragement or genuine questioning about the new skill can be very rewarding to the child.

To show respect: children will always learn about materials in individual ways and allowing them some control over how they will learn through investigation and experimentation offers respect for this individuality.

To offer help discreet offers of help to the child who has become frustrated can help move her forward in her work with new materials.

•••••••••••••••••••••• *Helpful hints* ••••••••••••••••••••••

| Do engage in genuine conversation with the child about her activities. Do offer praise and encouragement. | Don't dishearten children. Don't ridicule or correct children bluntly. |

To encourage independence: with encouragement children can become more and more self-reliant. Part of this learning involves being responsible for their own actions (as far as is practical). The adult needs to provide constant reassurance when helping a child to take on new responsibilities, for instance, learning to get dressed and undressed, learning to keep herself clean, helping to prepare for meals and clear away, getting snacks and simple cooking activities. These are all activities which encourage self-help skills and general social development. Adults need to encourage children to clear up and these sessions may provide opportunities for matching and sorting activities.

To observe: the early years worker needs to be alert to noting the emergence of new skills or any frustrations and to plan accordingly.

•••••••••••••••••••••• *Helpful hints* ••••••••••••••••••••••

| A child in a wheelchair should have access to any materials offered to all children. However, some equipment may need to be modified. Adults should ensure that their expectations of a child with disabilities are based | on objective and not subjective observation. Expectations should not be too low, which might hold the child back, or too high, which might lead to the child becoming frustrated. |

To join in: adults must be positive role models who listen carefully and ensure fairness and equality, for instance, a man can organise a cooking activity or a woman could join in a woodwork session. 'Joining-in' also offers adults the opportunity to maintain safety standards, to ensure that no child is left out and to encourage non-competitive games.

• *Helpful hints* •

Beware of transmitting stereotypical images of what boys and girls can achieve. The early years worker is a powerful role model who needs to be aware of the messages they are transmitting.

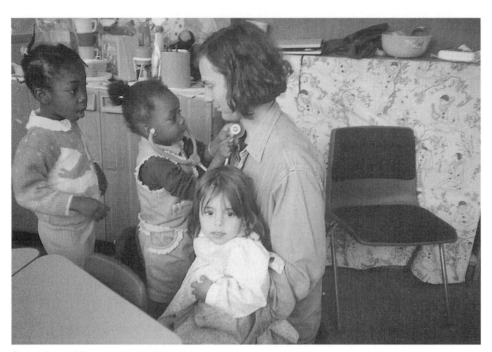

An adult providing a positive role model

Summary

▶ It is necessary to observe and assess in order to plan for activities.
▶ It is necessary to use a variety of materials to ensure a wide range of experiences.
▶ During activities, the role of the adult includes: offering encouragement, showing enthusiasm, providing attention, showing respect, helping at appropriate moments and joining in.

18

Theories on Child Development

Aims of the chapter

► To introduce the reader to a selection of theorists
► to give a brief outline of some of the theories on aspects of children's development researched by well-known theorists
► to provide the reader with a reading list should they wish to study a particular theory in depth.

The theorists

The following information is arranged alphabetically for simplicity and is not in order of priority. It is not intended to be an exhaustive list of theorists and the authors are not recommending any one theory as being more important than another.

•••••••••••••••••••••• *Helpful hint* ••••••••••••••••••••

It is important to recognise that many researchers have concentrated their research in Western society and therefore some theories have yet to be tested in other societies.

Why Study?
- understanding the needs of the child
- understanding holistic development
- understanding norms of development

Observing, Recordkeeping and Taking Action
- the value of observing
- different methods used
- importance of record keeping
- when to take action

Theories on Child Development
- introduces a selection of theorists
- briefly outlines some theories
- suggested reading

ENCOURAGING HOLISTIC DEVELOPMENT

Child Development Birth to eleven months
- motor skills
- hearing and vision
- language, cognition and symbolic development
- emotional and social development

Activities
- the value of observing and assessing
- importance of materials
- role of the adult

Child Development Four years to seven years and eleven months
- motor skills
- language, cognition and symbolic development
- emotional and social development

Child Development One year to three years and eleven months
- motor skills
- language, cognition and symbolic development
- emotional and social development

Name	Dates	Location	Area of study	Main theories	Comments
Mary Ainsworth	Experimented in the 1960s	UK	Attachment	• she experimented by measuring babies' responses to strangers when they were with their mothers, on their own, and then reunited with their mothers • she used the term the 'sensitive mother' to describe mothers who respond promptly to the needs of their babies.	• she worked with Bowlby (see p. 00) • she contributed to the debate about responsiveness and trust between mother and baby

Name	Dates	Location	Area of study	Main theories	Comments
Chris Athey	Researched in the 1970s	UK	Schemas	• she believes that a schema is 'a pattern of repeatable behaviour into which experiences are assimilated and that are gradually coordinated.' (Athey 1990, p. 37) • she believes that there are two avenues of child development schemas: biological and socio-cultural aspects of development	• her understanding of schemas has contributed to the work of early years workers during observation work and has served to inform curriculum planning • Cathy Nutbrown (1994) discussed the importance of the adult's descriptive language supporting the child's schemas. She built on the work of Chris Athey

Name	Dates	Location	Area of study	Main theories	Comments
Dr. John Bowlby	Researched from 1950s to 1970s	UK	Attachment	• he thought that early attachment was very important • mother and baby relationships very important • babies need one central figure/carer • children separated from their families in hospitals/institutions went through stages of loss and grief	• he was influenced by the research of James and Joyce Robertson • it is now thought that babies can develop relationships with more than one person • his work led to the introduction of key-workers • Bowlby's work also led to changes in the treatment of children in hospitals/institutions

Name	Dates	Location	Area of study	Main theories	Comments
Jerome Bruner	Researched from 1960s to 1990s	USA and UK	Social constructivism	• Bruner believed that adults can greatly help the development of children's thinking • he believed that children learn by doing • he identified enactive thinking, iconic thinking, symbolic thinking and discussed 'scaffolding' as a way in which the adult can help develop a child's thinking	• Jerome Bruner's background is psychology • he developed Vygotsky's concept of the zone of proximal development

Name	Dates	Location	Area of study	Main theories	Comments
Noam Chomsky	Researched in the 1960s	USA	Language	• children are born with an innate capacity for language development. He called this Language Acquisition Device • human beings possess this predisposition to listen, talk and learn	• Chomsky contributed to the debate on language development

Name	Dates	Location	Area of study	Main theories	Comments
Erik H Erikson	Researched in the 1950s and 1960s	UK	Development of personality	• he was concerned with the superego and how society influences a child's development • he was influenced by Freud's work on the theory of personality	• he contributed to psychodynamic theories of development

Name	Dates	Location	Area of study	Main theories	Comments
Sigmund Freud	Researched – Most productive period of psychoanalytical theory 1900–1930, although some revision after this date	Austria and UK	Personality development	• he was the founder of psychoanalytical theory and immensely influential in twentieth century theories of personality development • he believed that experiences in early childhood have a profound influence on the personality and adult life • Freud identified different personality components as an 'id', an 'ego' and a 'superego'	• his theories have always been regarded as controversial • he believed that his theories represented a major breakthrough in understanding development of personality

Name	Dates	Location	Area of study	Main theories	Comments
Friedrich Froebel	Experimented in the early years of the nineteenth century	Germany	How children learn	• he expressed the importance of children having real experiences including being physically active • Froebel thought of schools as communities which included parents, whom he recognised as being the first educators of their children • he encouraged music and movement indoors and outdoors • he encouraged an appreciation of arts, crafts and literature in addition to mathematical understanding • he thought that a child's best thinking is done when they are playing • he emphasised the importance of relationships and feelings with other children as well as adults	• Froebel has had a long-term influence on the education and care of young children

Name	Dates	Location	Area of study	Main theories	Comments
Harry and Margaret Harlow	Experimented in the 1960s and 1970s	USA	Attachment	• they carried out experiments on monkeys using isolating techniques and surrogate mothers • they concluded that contact and comfort is critical to emotional and social development • they also concluded that there was a sensitive period of six months and if the monkeys were isolated for any longer they would never recover • the release of the isolated monkeys into the company of 'normally reared' monkeys caused their behaviour to be so badly disturbed that they could not join in normal rough and tumble games and engaged in self-harm	• Bowlby drew conclusions concerning Harlow's experiments of maternal and social privation

Name	Dates	Location	Area of study	Main theories	Comments
Susan Isaacs	Researched in the 1920s and 1930s	UK	Emotional expression	• observing children and valuing play as a means through which they can express their feelings • she encouraged a nursery type of education until children were about seven years old	• she was influenced by the work of Froebel and Melanie Klein

Name	Dates	Location	Area of study	Main theories	Comments
Lawrence Kolberg	Researched from 1950s to 1980s	USA	Moral reasoning	• Kolberg extended Piaget's theories on moral reasoning • he identified six stages of moral reasoning in three levels: Level 1: Pre-conventional morality Level 2: Conventional morality Level 3: Post-conventional morality	• Kolberg was interested in the way children reason and justify their moral judgements • Kolberg does not tie his stages of moral reasoning to particular ages

Name	Dates	Location	Area of study	Main theories	Comments
Konrad Lorenz	Experimented in the 1930s	Austria	Attachment and imprinting	• investigated the origins of baby animals' attachment to their carers • he was the first to investigate imprinting – a very rapid form of attachment • when studying goslings, Lorenz found that there was a sensitive period during the first few hours after hatching when the gosling would 'fix' on the first moving figure it saw. He called this 'fixation' imprinting.	• he was a pioneer in the science of ethology • Hess conducted more formal studies resulting from Lorenz's conclusions • Bowlby used the work of Konrad Lorenz

Name	Dates	Location	Area of study	Main theories	Comments
Margaret McMillan	Researched from 1900 to 1930s	UK	The development of nursery schools	• she encouraged partnership with parents • she emphasised the importance of good nourishment and health	• pioneering influence on school meals and medical services

Name	Dates	Location	Area of study	Main theories	Comments
Abraham Maslow	Researched in the 1950s and 1960s	USA	Motivation	• he described a hierarchy of needs through which individuals tend to move in search of personal fulfilment. The needs at each level must be partially met before the individual is motivated to move to the next level.	• the theory is widely used in training staff in business management, health and social care

Name	Dates	Location	Area of study	Main theories	Comments
Maria Montessori	Researched early 1900s	Italy	Learning	• that children are particularly receptive to certain areas of learning during sensitive periods of learning • She constructed 'didactic' materials to encourage children to use their hands	• her work was built on many hours of observing children

Name	Dates	Location	Area of study	Main theories	Comments
Ivan Pavlov	Researched late 1800s	Russia	Classical conditioning	• Pavlov conducted experiments mainly on dogs and identified behaviour in response to stimuli. He referred to these types of behaviour as classical conditioning	• Pavlov was a physiologist • Louis Lipsitt (1990) conducted experiments which supported Pavlov's findings

Name	Dates	Location	Area of study	Main theories	Comments
Jean Piaget	Researched from 1920s to 1970s	Switzerland	Constructivism, Cognitive development Moral development, Discovery learning, Language development	• he was interested in the similarities between children • he showed that children actively construct their understanding of the world by interacting with it. He believed that logical thinking developed in steps: 0–2 years sensori-motor period; 2–7 years pre-operational period; 7–11 years concrete operations; 11–adult formal operations • he described mental structures and called them schemas • he developed a new method of investigation – 'the storytelling method' – and drew conclusions about children's understanding of intentions and consequences	• he considered his work as a natural outgrowth of his biological studies • he did not think that intelligence was fixed at birth • Piaget made a great contribution to our understanding of cognitive development

Name	Dates	Location	Area of study	Main theories	Comments
Mia Kellmer Pringle	Researched 1960s to 1970s	UK	Children's fundamental needs	• she built on the work of Maslow (1962) and Susan Isaacs (1968) • she stressed the importance of intrinsic motivation based on the quality of a child's early social relationships	• she was pioneer director of the National Children's Bureau • Kellmer Pringle stressed the central importance of a child's health and living conditions in relation to educational needs

Name	Dates	Location	Area of study	Main theories	Comments
Sir Michael Rutter	Research mainly from 1970s onwards	London and Isle of Wight	Nature/nuture debate, Family break up	• he considers that there is a correlation between the amount of stress in the child's background and the likelihood of the child becoming deviant • he considers learning is 60 percent nature and 40 percent nurture	• he concludes that early separation need not have lasting ill effects, but he was less optimistic about the future of children who never made affectionate bonds

Name	Dates	Location	Area of study	Main theories	Comments
B F Skinner	Researched in the 1930s	USA	Operant conditioning	• conducted experiments with stimuli and positive and negative reinforcements • he identified these responses as operant conditioning	• Chomsky (1960s) challenged Skinner's theories and carried out experiments which showed that language development is not a result of operant conditioning • behaviour therapy is based on operant conditioning methods

Name	Dates	Location	Area of study	Main theories	Comments
Barbara Tizard	Research in 1970s with Judith Rees and Jill Hodges	UK	Attachment	• her studies showed that children are capable of forming close attachments to 'new mothers' even at a late age	• her research contributed to the debate over the idea of a sensitive period • her research showed that adoption can be a very satisfactory arrangement

Name	Dates	Location	Area of study	Main theories	Comments
Lev Vygotsky	Researched 1920s	Russia	Social constructivism	• Vygotsky believed that the child is an active constructor of knowledge and understanding • the main features of his theory are the zone of proximal development • he discussed the importance of internalising social interactions • he discussed the importance of play as a way in which children reach the zone of proximal development • he considered that the social and cultural context were crucial to a child's learning	

Name	Dates	Location	Area of study	Main theories	Comments
D W Winnicott	Research 1960s	UK	Attachment	• he believed that play was essential to emotional and social development • he believed that the child's capacity to learn is directly related to the developmental stages in a child's play • he identified comforters to which children become especially attached as being important transitional objects	• Winnicott contributed to ideas on symbolic thinking

Summary

▶ The reader has been introduced to a selection of theorists.
▶ A brief outline of some of the theories on aspects of children's development researched by well-known theorists have been provided.
▶ Further reading can be found in the References and Bibliography.

Summary of Part 5

▶ It is necessary to observe and assess in order to plan for activities.
▶ it is necessary to use a variety of materials to ensure a wide range of experiences
▶ during activities the role of the adult includes offering encouragement, showing enthusiasm, providing attention, showing respect, helping at appropriate moments and joining in
▶ the reader has been introduced to a selection of theorists
▶ a brief outline of some of the theories on aspects of children's development researched by well known theorists have been provided
▶ further reading can be found in the References and Bibliography.

Suggestions for Further Reading

Athey, C. (1990) *Extending Thought in Young Children: A Parent-Teacher Partnership*. Paul Chapman Publishing, London.

Bee, H. (1992) *The Developing Child*. Harper Collins Publishers, New York.

Brierley, J. (1994) *Give me a Child Until he is Seven: Brain Studies and Early Childhood Education*, 2nd edition. The Falmer Press, London.

Bruce, T. and Meggitt, C. (1996) *Child Care and Education*. Hodder and Stoughton, London.

Bruce, T. (1999) *Early Childhood Education*, 2nd edition. Hodder and Stoughton, London.

Bruner, J.S. (1963) *The Process of Education*. Vintage Books, New York.

Davenport, G.C. (1989) *An Introduction to Child Development*. Unwin Hyman Ltd, London.

Thomson, H. and Meggitt, C. (1997) *Human Growth and Development*. Hodder and Stoughton, London.

Vygotsky, L. (1986) *Thought and Language*. MIT, Cambridge (Mass.).

Bibliography

Athey, C. (1990) *Extending thought in young children: A parent–teacher partnership*. Paul Chapman Publishing, London.

Bee, H. (1992) *The Developing Child*. Harper Collins Publishers, New York.

Bruce, T. (1996) *Helping Children to Play*. Hodder and Stoughton, London.

Bruce, T. and Meggitt, C. (1996) *Child Care and Education*. Hodder and Stoughton, London.

Bruner, J. (1990) *Acts of Meaning*. Harvard University Press, Cambridge, M.A.

Chomsky, N. (1968) *Language and the Mind*. Harcourt, Brace and World, New York.

Davenport, G.C. (1989) *An Introduction to Child Development*. Unwin Hyman, London.

Donaldson, M. (1978) *Children's Minds*. Fortuna/Collins, London.

Drummond, M.J. (1993) *Assessing Children's Learning*. David Fulton, London.

Dunn, J. (1988) *The Beginnings of Social* Understanding. Blackwell, Oxford.

Elfer, P. 'Building Intimacy in Relationships with Young Children in Nurseries.' *Early Years TACTYC Journal*. Spring 1996

Geraghty, P. (1988) *Caring for Children*, 2nd edition. Ballière Tindall, London.

HMSO (1991) *Working Together Under The Children Act, 1989*. HMSO, London.

Harding, J. and Meldon-Smith, L. (1996) *How to Make Observations and Assessments*. Hodder and Stoughton, London.

Hall, D. (ed.) (1994) *The Child Surveillance Handbook*, 2nd edition. Radcliffe Medical Press, Oxford.

Lansdown, R. and Walker, M. (1991) *Your Child's Development From Birth to Adolescence*. Francis Lincoln Ltd, London.

Lindon, J. (1986) *Working with Young Children*, 3rd edition. Hodder and Stoughton, London.

Lindon, J. (1994) *Child Development from Birth to Eight. A Practical Focus*. National Children's Bureau, Derby.

Matterson, E.M. (1989) *Play with Purpose for the Under Sevens*. Penguin, Harmondsworth.

Middleton, L. (1992) *Children First – Working with Children and Disability*. Venture Press, Birmingham.

Nutbrown, C. (1994) *Threads of Learning*. Paul Chapman Publishing, London.

O'Hagan, M. and Smith, M. (1993) *Special Issues in Child Care*. Baillière Tindall, London.

Pearce, Dr J. (1994) *Growth and Development*. HarperCollins, London.

Petrie, P. (1987) *Baby Play*. Pantheon, London.

Piaget, J. (1962) *Play, Dreams and Imitation in Childhood*. Routledge and Kegan Paul, London.

Pugh, G. (ed.) (1992) *Contemporary Issues in the Early Years: Working Collaboratively for Children*. Paul Chapman Publishing, London.

Sinclair, D. (1990) *Human Growth after Birth*. Oxford University Press, Oxford.

Siraj-Blachford, I. (1994) *The Early Years: Laying the Foundations for Racial Equality*. Trentham Books, Stoke on Trent.

Swain, J. (ed.) (1993) *Disabling Barriers, Enabling Environments*. Sage Publications.

Sylva, K. and Lunt, I. (1988) *Child Development. A First Course*. Blackwell, Oxford.

Thomson, H. and Meggitt, C. (1997) *Human Growth and Development*. Hodder and Stoughton, London.

Whalley, M. (1994) *Learning to be Strong: Integrating Education and Care in Early Childhood*. Hodder and Stoughton, London.

Useful Addresses

Action for Sick Children
Argyle House
29–31 Euston Road
London NW1 2SD
Tel: 0171 833 2041

Advisory Centre for Education
1b Aberdeen Studios
22 Highbury Grove
London N5 2EA
Tel: 0171 354 8321

AFASIC – Overcoming Speech Impairments
347 Central Markets
Smithfield
London EC1A 9NH
Tel: 0171 236 3632/6487

British Diabetic Association
10 Queen Anne Street
London W1M 0BD
Tel: 0171 323 1531

British Dyslexia Association
98 London Road
Reading RG1 5AU
Tel: 01734 668271

British Epilepsy Association
Anstey House
40 Hanover Square
Leeds LS3 1BE
Tel: 01132 439393

Hyperactive Children Support Group
71 Whyke Lane
Chichester
Sussex PO19 2LD
Tel: 01903 725182

MENCAP
117–123 Golden Lane
London EC1Y ORT
Tel: 0171 454 0454

National Asthma Campaign
Providence Place
Providence House
London N1 0NT
Tel: 0171 226 2260

National Autistic Society
276 Willesden Lane
London NW2 5RB
Tel: 0181 451 1114

National Children's Bureau
8 Wakely Street
London EC1V 7QE
Tel: 0171 843 6000

National Deaf Children Society
15 Dufferin Street
London EC1Y 8PD
Tel: 0171 250 0123

**The Royal National Institute
for the Blind**
224 Great Portland Street
London W1N 6AA
Tel: 0171 388 1266

Scope
6 Market Road
London N7 9PW
Tel: 0171 619 7100

Sickle Cell Society
54 Station Road
London NW10 4UA
Tel: 0181 961 7795